INTEGRATED DEFENSIVE FIGHTING SYSTEMS, INC.

PRESENTS

F.I.G.H.T.

Fierce Israeli Guerilla Hand-to-hand Tactics Combat Proven and Battle Tested

#K-518-1996

Volume One

Hand-To-Hand Combat
AS TAUGHT BY ISRAELI SPECIAL FORCES

Developed by Mike Lee Kanarek
Written by Randy S. Proto
Edited by John Exum
Illustrations by Carlos Gelpi

Dedication

This manual is dedicated to the surviving and fallen freedom fighters of the Israel Defense Forces, including the brave Haganah members, the IDF's predecessor.

Special thanks go to my direct commanders during my service in the IDF Special Operations Group 'Orev Golani'. Without their leadership, graduating my 'Masloul' would not have been possible. Their faith in selecting and training me will be treasured and deeply appreciated forever.

Also, professional appreciation goes to my fellow Israeli born instructors: Moti Horenstein, Rhon Mizrachi and Nir Maman. While the Haganah system and the F.I.G.H.T. program have become a modern creation of their own, their unselfish contribution of their arts: Hisardut, Krav Maga, KAPAP, and LOTAR have been instrumental in the making of my system.

There remains a small group of people, whose names, units or associations with me I cannot list for security reasons. These operators are still active in their elite units in the war against terrorism. You know who you are- TODA!

Mike Lee Kanarek
Chief Instructor Haganah- USA
Creator of the F.I.G.H.T. Training Series
October 1, 2002, Weston, Florida

Product Liability Disclaimer
And Notice Of Inherent Dangers
READ BEFORE USE

assumes no responsibility or liability regarding the safety of your training or the consequences of your use of these techniques;

7) IDFS and its officers, shareholders, directors, employees, and affiliated persons and entities assume no responsibility or liability for any injury caused by the use of any of the techniques shown in this manual, including but not limited to, injuries sustained by third parties that are not party to this agreement; and

8) You will not instruct anyone on the techniques shown in this manual unless you are a certified martial arts instructor, in which case, while this is not an authorization or license to teach the techniques, you assume any and all responsibility for such instruction and IDFS and its officers, shareholders, directors, employees, and affiliated persons and entities assume no responsibility or liability;

Table Of Contents

How To Use This Book With The F.I.G.H.T. Video/DVD Series

This book is designed to be a training guide in simple, effective, combat and street-proven self-defense techniques. It can be used effectively on its own, or in conjunction with the F.I.G.H.T. DVD or VHS series, which may be purchased online at *www.fight2survive.com*. To facilitate using it with the videos, each major section in the book is cross referenced to both the VHS and DVD series. In the side column on the page where a given topic begins there is a box that looks like this:

REFERENCE
Video Tape: **1**
◄ Section: **3.0**
DVD: **2**
Volume: **2**
Menu Chapter: **4**
◄ Section: **4.1**

The box will refer to a VHS video number and section, and a DVD number, volume, chapter number, and section. In this example, the box directs you to VHS 1 (the first of the 5 tapes in the series) and on that tape to section 3.0. Each section on the tape is labeled onscreen in the lower right-hand corner. You would simply insert VHS tape 1 and Fast Forward to Section 3.0. Likewise, the example directs you to DVD 2, Volume 2, chapter 4, section 4.1. In this case, you would insert DVD #2 (of 3 in the series), view the introductory material, and then bring up the menu for volume 2, click on chapter 4 and then when chapter 4 starts playing, fast forward to section 4.1.

Mike is a former Israeli Special Operations Group Commando of the battle-hardened Golani Brigade and a world class Hand-to-Hand Combat instructor. His hard-core small team Special Ops unit operated behind enemy lines typically alone and miles from backup. In south Lebanon they terminated terrorists and destroyed their headquarters. In the West Bank during the first Intifada they went house to house capturing key militants and controlling street riots. Extreme violence was daily routine. Mike brings to the table this knowledge and his 20 years of full contact martial arts experience to teach you to devastate an attacker fast.

Born Lee Van Hong in Saigon in 1967 to a Vietnamese mother and an American father proudly serving his country during the Vietnam War, at age six months Mike was adopted by a Jewish family in Belgium and given the name Michel Kanarek. In 1977, Michel's father, Emil Kanarek, moved his family to Israel. He had been a volunteer soldier in the Israeli Independence War in 1948, belonging to the "Palmach Brigades" in one of the "Haganah" units (the Haganah system is named in his honor). His regiment freed Jerusalem in that war. Between the ages of 6 and 18, Mike studied judo and then karate until joining the IDF at age 18 in 1985. After serving three years as a Special Forces member in Orev Golani (one of the most elite commando units in the IDF) where he was extensively trained in KAPAP among other combative methodologies and technologies, Mike was honorably discharged as an outstanding soldier. He then worked as a high profile security professional for a private Israeli security company until he could afford to immigrate to the United States. For more than 10 years since arriving in the United States Mike has taught combat based self defense skills to civilians, military and law enforcement professionals, including Secret Service, FBI and DEA agents, SWAT team members, Navy SEALS, and many local law enforcement professionals. He regularly provides specialty courses in Israeli Combat Shooting, Counter Terrorist Tactics,

Israeli Tactical Knife Fighting and many specially requested private courses. He is a survivor of many unarmed engagements and lives with gunshot and knife wounds. In addition to his hand-to-hand and 'hot' weapons expertise, he is a respected specialist in tactical knife applications.

In addition to his military training in KAPAP and more recent training in LOTAR, Mike Lee Kanarek has trained under Mr. Joe Lewis for nearly 10 years, and is a fifth degree black belt in Joe Lewis American Full Contact Karate. He holds a fourth degree black belt in Survival Hisardut under Moti Horenstein, Muay Thai King Cup Super Heavyweight World Champion and SHIDOKAN Super Heavyweight U.S. Champion. He holds a first degree black belt in Krav Maga under Rhon Mizrachi, the highest ranking most experienced Israeli IDF veteran Krav Maga instructor in the U.S. as of this writing. Mike is a fully certified Muay Thai Kickboxing instructor and holds other belts, including a blue belt in Brazilian Jiu-Jitsu. He has been recognized as The Self-Defense Instructor of the Year by the Florida Martial Arts Brotherhood Hall of Fame and has numerous other awards and recognitions.

His passion is bringing together the best elements of various practical combat fighting arts as taught by world-class instructors, adding militarily tested elements, and teaching them to law abiding citizens in the fastest most effective way possible to enable them to come home safe each day. He has seen more violence than anyone should have to, and has learned how to overcome it. He brings that experience to you.

Thank you for purchasing the F.I.G.H.T. self-defense manual. While not necessary, for your added benefit if you haven't already done so, we encourage you to purchase the F.I.G.H.T. series of videos or DVDs that go along with this manual. They demonstrate all the techniques included in this manual, and more. The F.I.G.H.T. video/DVD series as well as other videos/DVD and seminar information, are available by going to *www.fight2survive.com*.

The F.I.G.H.T. program uses Haganah, the most effective self-defense system available today. Haganah literally translates as "Defense". The Haganah self-defense system is primarily a merger of the two official martial arts of Israel, Krav Maga and Hisardut, added military tactics taught in KAPAP and LOTAR and other hand-to-hand and armed fighting techniques used by Israeli Special Forces operatives in extremely hostile situations. Haganah carefully combines the best elements of these disciplines into a devastating street-combat system. One of the most powerful aspects of this combination of these disciplines in Haganah is its focus on getting to just a few specific common positions, called points of reference, from which a common set of techniques can be employed, depending upon your ultimate objective in the engagement. This structure allows you to develop sound skills very quickly because it minimizes the number of unique counterattacks you must learn to be effective.

Ground fighting is not an objective of the system because it is ineffective in multiple attacker scenarios, exposes you to knife deployment in a tactically bad situation and is damaging to both parties on most terrain. However, some fights end up on the ground, so Haganah combines ground fighting techniques of the two best systems in the world – Brazilian Jiu-Jitsu and Russian Sambo- with Israeli Special Forces techniques into its ground survival strategy. The sole goal of the ground survival component of Haganah is to dominate and damage your adversary and get back up off the ground as quickly as possible. It is available in a separate set of F.I.G.H.T. DVD/VHS and a separate manual on our website.

Elite seminars with former Israeli commandos certified in Haganah are available. Typically, there is a wait for an available slot in a seminar. We encourage you to enroll in a seminar and, prior to attending, to study this manual and the videos in order to develop an understanding of the techniques. While you can achieve a good level of preparedness by diligently studying and practicing the material in the manual and videos, there is no substitute for in-person training. The combination of individual study and seminar participation or enrollment at an Authorized F.I.G.H.T. Training Center brings you to another level. Seminar information and a list of authorized training centers is available on our website.

As proponents of effective self-defense methodologies we recommend that you learn both tactical knife fighting and combat (not target!) shooting in addition to the hand-to-hand techniques presented in this manual, and that to the extent permitted by law, you carry a knife. In fact, we believe that if you, as a civilian, had to choose between carrying a knife or a gun, you should carry a knife. The Haganah system's techniques are designed to assume that your attacker has a knife (more criminals do than have guns), but empty hand defense is never as good as having an equal weapon. Consult the law for your locality to determine what, if any, weapon you are permitted to carry, and under what circumstances you are permitted to do so. We encourage you to learn to shoot even if you don't own or carry a gun if for no other reason than to understand what to do if you disarm an attacker who had a gun. Individuals interested in either tactical knife fighting training or combat shooting training please visit our website at *www.fight2survive.com*.

Finally, law enforcement or military personnel are extensively trained to deal with violent situations and sometimes confront them on a daily basis. If you work in these professions, you must evaluate everything in the F.I.G.H.T. system in accordance with your department's or unit's rules of engagement.

The Haganah system (and its components) was born out of a need to enable a state (or person) at a disadvantage – such as size or degree of armament – to defeat an adversary that had an advantage.

Since it's declaration of statehood in 1948, Israel (which smaller in both size and population than many states in the U.S.) has been under constant military and terrorist attack. As a result of constant engagement in a variety of settings, and its ability to defeat much larger opponents, the Israel Defense Forces (IDF) is considered by many one of the best Armies in the world today. Special Forces members of the IDF are regarded around the globe as top of the line, due to their extensive hands-on combat experience. The techniques incorporated into the system have been proven in violent hand-to-hand combat situations in Israel and have been carefully adapted to common street attacks.

The Haganah system is far from being an ordinary martial art. It is the wave of the future in hand-to-hand combat and street fighting methodologies. One of the most important features of the Haganah system is that, unlike many traditional martial arts systems, it is continuously enhanced. The IDF periodically updates its hand-to-hand combat techniques based on its daily combat experience. Haganah integrates these updates after adapting them, if necessary, for use by civilians and law enforcement professionals. Additionally, Haganah constantly evaluates other methodologies, such as those used by the various U.S. Special Forces, to take any techniques which they have which strengthen the system and add them in. There is no ego in the Haganah system. The Haganah System uses the best of the best in self defense and combat methodologies.

Haganah includes the following components, some of which are limited access – requiring active duty or veteran military or law enforcement status or background checks and approval by IDFS:

Techniques of Self-Defense:
- Defense against punches and kicks
- Escapes and releases from chokes, bear hugs and other grappling techniques
- Defense against cold weapons; knives, clubs, etc.
- Defense against hot weapons; guns, other firearms, automatic weapons and grenades
- Defense against multiple attackers

Hand-to-Hand Combat:
- Various types of arm blows including all hand parts, arms, and elbows
- Various types of kicks including all foot parts with/without shoes, and knees
- Ground survival techniques including combat-neutralizing grappling techniques, pinching, tendon and muscle tearing, and hardcore submission techniques

Israeli Tactical Knife Fighting

Israeli Combat Shooting

Counter-Terrorist Strategies and Techniques

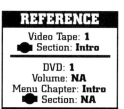

REFERENCE
Video Tape: **1**
◆ Section: **Intro**

DVD: **1**
Volume: **NA**
Menu Chapter: **Intro**
◆ Section: **NA**

METHOD OF TRAINING

Unlike many other systems which teach according to a belt level curriculum, adding techniques according to the rank level and seniority of the student, Haganah utilizes a military format. At its core, there are two carefully picked sets of the most common street attacks to work against. The first set of 20 techniques consists of empty-hand strategies addressing unarmed assailants. The second set of 18 techniques consists of unarmed self-defense strategies against knife attacks and threats at gun point. These two sets are taught in parallel in a four month rotation system.

This method has been proven very effective as a tool to train people quickly to be able to deploy the Haganah system in combative situations upon completing only four months of training. Our practitioners are exposed to the entire core system in that time. They have learned and trained in what would have been reserved in other more traditionally structured systems as advance material.

What makes this possible is our application of the Israeli KAPAP/LOTAR systems to the self-defense techniques. KAPAP is a Hebrew acronym for "Face to Face Combat", what is referred in the U.S. as "Hand to Hand Combat". LOTAR is the Hebrew combination of two words Lochama and Terror which directly translate to anti-terrorism warfare. KAPAP encompasses both a system of teaching and specific content as used in the Israeli military, where ordinary civilians (all Israelis serve in the military for 3 years) are turned into capable fighters in a matter of months, ready to confront life and death engagements. LOTAR encompasses both a system of teaching and specific content used to teach advanced urban and other combat tactics to Israeli Special Forces quickly. Both KAPAP and LOTAR focus on developing soldier's ability to accomplish specific objectives. The speed of training is accomplished with the Haganah system is due to its focus on achieving certain common objectives. Regardless of the initial attack, the Haganah system leads practitioners to one of three points of references, each with three objective options, where practitioners will be able to apply their skills. We call this approach the "Funnel."

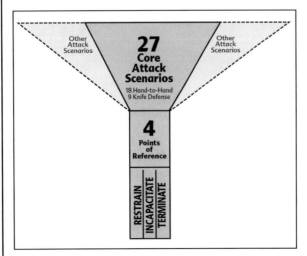

No matter the initial attack, you end up in one of a few common destination points (Points of Reference) and choose one of three options from there (Objective Options). By limiting the variety of combat strategies, learning time is accelerated and depth of understanding and skill levels are increased.

By practicing the techniques as explained in the 'Practicing' section of this manual (and particularly if you get the DVDs or videos), you can begin to have useable skills in a few weeks and achieve deployable skills in the 3 to 4 month timeframe.

While we do not issue or focus on rank, for their own evaluation of skill practitioners can be "ranked" according to their skill level in Haganah, including, at the advanced level, their skills in armed self defense. Mere seniority and accumulation of more techniques do not automatically rate a practitioner higher. Students must demonstrate skills in full contact situations. Only one belt can be achieved solely as a form of recognition of expert level status – Black Belt. To give you an idea of rankings and how much time would typically be required to achieve each:

- **Level** I – student exposed to all techniques and principles, demonstrates ability to apply them in controlled setting and demonstrates ability to apply point of reference techniques in a reactive setting (unplanned)
  – First Rotation, or completion of F.I.G.H.T. manual and video series and attending Level I seminar.

- **Level II** – student demonstrates an ability to identify and respond to an attack in a controlled setting and reactive highly stressed setting with effective entry and point of reference techniques, but in a reactive setting may improvise in sub-optimal ways
  – Second to Third Rotation, or completion of F.I.G.H.T. manual and video series, ground survival video series and Level I and II seminar

- **Level** III– student demonstrates ability to correctly identify and effectively respond to different types of attacks including unfamiliar sequences in a highly stressed reactive setting and demonstrates basic competence in combat shooting and knife fighting.
  – Fourth to Fifth Rotation, or completion of all F.I.G.H.T. videos (including Ground Survival, Tactical Knife Fighting and Combat Shooting and Level I, II, and III seminars (Level III seminar is limited access)

- **Expert Level** – practitioner is able to effectively defeat unrehearsed unique combinations of attacks from a Master Level Instructor, including defending from an inferior position and successfully engaging knife on knife. The student is able to clearly explain and demonstrate all techniques, including effective combat shooting techniques.
  – Six to Eight Rotations, or at least one rotation completion of all Advanced Level F.I.G.H.T. requirements, at least one additional limited access seminar (such as Counter Terrorist)

- **Master Level** – is only available to instructors who go beyond the expert level and make contributions to the enhancement of the system itself. Master Level instructors must have been engaged in actual hand-to-hand or armed combat situations.

F.I.G.H.T.
Principles And Combatives

MINDSET

If you have never been violently attacked, you are lucky. If you have, what we are about to say will not surprise you. Most attacks include 'verbal violence' designed to shock you or establish your attacker's dominance. Imagine you are just about to get into your car when a person grabs you from behind, puts a knife to your throat and says "Don't say shit. You're coming with me you fucking asshole, or I'll kill you." When this occurs, several things will happen. You will experience terror. Your body will flood with adrenaline. Your muscles may 'lock up'. You will likely break out in a sweat all over, including your hands. Your mind will be momentarily blank. Your perception of time and distance will likely become distorted and your focus may tunnel in on what you see as the dominant threat. All of these things happen automatically and are part of your fundamental instinct to defend yourself by preparing to flee or fight.

When attacked, most of us react in ways that our instincts tell us are *protective*. Many of us want to flee the scene. This is not always possible. The key to surviving in a self-defense situation is to understand our instincts and go beyond them by programming ourselves to automatically react in ways that will be *effective*. Effectiveness in self defense is very straightforward- a defense is effective if it stops an attacker *and* prevents them from attacking again. Self defense isn't about pretty moves or showing off. It is about surviving violence. There is no way to know an attacker's ultimate intent. As long as a person is being attacked the attack can progress to the next level. Muggings turn into murders. Rapes turn into murders. It is likely that, if you are attacked by a criminal, he is armed. Although the news focuses on stories which involve guns, more petty criminals are armed with some type of knife. Knives are easier to obtain and conceal, the penalties associated with their possession are less severe, and they are as effective as guns in many situations. You will not know if your attacker is armed unless they announce it by displaying their weapon in a way that you can see it. In most knife attacks, the victim didn't realize there was a knife and that they had been stabbed until after it was over. Given all that you don't know when a self- defense situation erupts, there are only three ways to ensure survival and avoid unanticipated escalation when threatened:
- Avoid the situation
- Escape, or
- Devastate your attacker's ability to fight and then escape from the situation.

Always avoid violence if possible. Escape a threat-

ened attack if possible. Avoidance and escape come from awareness and a mindset that starts with a desire not to fight. Let's discuss those two things. First, awareness means noticing your surroundings. Most of us know when something does not feel right. Walking to our cars in a dark parking lot. Going down an alley. Meeting a stranger in a place where there are few other people. Be alert. Avoidance comes from adding specific strategies to your awareness of your surroundings. These range from communications strategies to try to diffuse a situation to active, action oriented strategies such as always leaving an escape route when in unfamiliar territory. There are many publications which deal with avoidance strategies. Particularly good information is available on our website *www.fight2survive.com* in the members area.

If you are caught off guard and are put in a situation that has not "become a fight" (we will talk about this later), then you should first decide if you can safely escape. Can you keep your distance and get to safety? This is a split second decision, and requires you to be aware enough of your surroundings to know if an escape route exists, if safety exists nearby and if you can keep your distance during your escape.

Finally, have a mindset that you really do not want to hit another person unless you have to, not out of fear of them but rather *because if you do hit them, you know you will devastate them*. This is an important concept. The F.I.G.H.T. mindset of 'avoidance or escape' as a preferred approach is not born out of fear of defeat, rather it is born out of a desire not to do the amount of damage you know you will have to do if the engagement actually occurs. Said another way, the F.I.G.H.T. mindset is:

I will do my best to avoid violence, but if attacked I will devastate my attacker with overwhelming <u>violence</u>.

You will learn many self-defense and fighting techniques in this manual. They are all designed to be used with the intent to devastate your attacker. Devastate typically means incapacitate. That is – damage him enough so the attacker cannot continue his attack. In the least threatening circumstance, it can also mean restrain, but only if you are confident for some reason that you can in fact end the encounter by simply restraining your attacker, or you are required to do so as a professional. However, in the most extreme situation, where your life is in imminent danger, it can also mean terminate your attacker. You choose between these three objectives. If this mindset appears harsh,

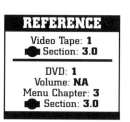

REFERENCE

Video Tape: **1**
◆ Section: **3.0**

DVD: **1**
Volume: **NA**
Menu Chapter: **3**
◆ Section: **3.0**

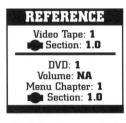

REFERENCE

Video Tape: **1**
Section: **1.0**

DVD: **1**
Volume: **NA**
Menu Chapter: **1**
Section: **1.0**

REFERENCE

Video Tape: **1**
Section: **2.0**

DVD: **1**
Volume: **NA**
Menu Chapter: **2**
Section: **2.0**

here is a scenario to consider. You are grabbed from behind. Your attacker is pulling you backwards. It is dark. Depending upon who you are, he is using every racial or sexual slur and certainly every vulgar word you can imagine. At the same time, he is telling you to cooperate. What can you be sure of? You don't know:

- If he is armed
- If he is bigger, stronger or more skilled than you
- If he is alone
- Where he is trying to take you
- What his intended level of violence is. Regardless of what he says- why would you trust him? Will it be to rob only, beat, rape (male and females get raped), cut, kill?
- And a lot more.

There is only one thing you do know: that he does not care at all about your life.

Whatever he intends to do, he has already taken your peace of mind and forcibly damaged your life. DO NOT LET HIM DO WORSE! The F.I.G.H.T. system focuses on devastation because of the many unknowns in a violent encounter. It will not work like in the movies. Because of all of the unknowns, you have to stop this attack fast and make damn sure your attacker cannot get up and come back for more. No matter how skilled you are, you are not superhuman. There is always someone better than you. And, if you are unskilled your attacker starts out more capable than you. You must assume that he can win if you give him the chance. You owe him little. You have one decision to make. Will you let him live? That decision depends totally on the situation. Is he visibly armed? Are you reasonably certain that if you did not terminate him, he would attempt to take your life? *Is there any way to escape without risking your life?* Different jurisdictions have different laws regarding killing in self-defense, whether with a weapon or with your hands. We cannot and do not tell you what is permitted, you must study the laws of your state, but what we can and do say is don't hesitate to fight for your life when it is threatened and you cannot run. As soon as you feel that the assault has begun and you are physically endangered - EXPLODE.

PRINCIPLES

1. *Avoid getting hit.* Techniques will always have an element that minimizes the danger of you being hit, especially in your vulnerable areas.

2. *Don't be fancy.* Techniques are simple and do not conflict with natural or instinctive body movements..

3. *Defend yourself in the quickest, safest and most effective way.* Most techniques include both defensive and offensive elements designed to protect you while inflicting maximum possible damage to your opponent to end the conflict quickly.

4. *Use the opponent's vulnerable and weak points.* The groin, throat, eyes and other sensitive parts of the body are your primary targets. Techniques are designed to also exploit the many other not so obvious weak points on the human body.

5. *Don't rely on strength.* Techniques are designed to minimize your effort, enabling you to work effectively even when at a size, strength or position disadvantage.

6. *Use available objects as weapons.* The system is designed to teach you to effectively use improvised and ordinary weapons.

7. *If forced to fight, no rules, no limits.* If diplomacy fails, no hesitation, no holding back - anything goes.

CONCEPTS AND TERMINOLOGY

As you progress through the F.I.G.H.T. program, certain concepts will be used repeatedly. You will read (and see in the videos) certain terms repeatedly. An overview of both is presented here.

Every counter attack technique has three elements: defense, offense, and footwork. Each strike has a component that is designed to protect you, such as raising an arm or turning your body in a certain direction. Each strike also has defined the proper footwork which either makes the defensive or offensive element more effective, or positions you for a particular category of subsequent strikes. And, each strike has a component that is designed to damage your opponent. It is important that you perform all three components effectively.

DIA. 1

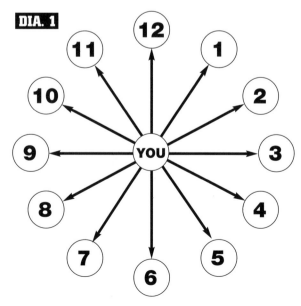

In describing proper footwork and positioning, we will use a 'clock' concept. You will always be at the center of the clock. Assuming your opponent is straight in front of you, he is at 12 o'clock. If you were to move to 11 o'clock you would take a walking step with both legs to your left and forward as shown in the **Diagram 1**. The "clock" is used as an abbreviation.

Each technique is designed to be used at a specific range, i.e. distance between you and your attacker. We generally refer to four ranges:

- **No man's land**. Neither of you can reach the other.
- **Long range**. You can reach each other's body with kicks, but not your hands.
- **Middle range**. You can reach each other's body with your hands.
- **Close (Clinch) range**. Your bodies are touching or are within a few inches of each other.

Right handers and left handers may perform each technique differently. Generally the techniques are pictured from the perspective of a right hander but described using more generic terms such as: strong side, weak side, outside, inside, front or rear. Your strong side is the side of your dominant hand (weak side is opposite). Front and rear are obvious. The inside means closest to the centerline of your attacker's or your body (depending upon the context) and outside means furthest from the centerline.

There is a psychological relationship between the parties at the outset of a violent encounter. It is very simple- one views himself as a predator, one as a victim. When you are attacked, you are definitely _a_ victim. That's OK; it is the unfortunate reality of being attacked. You just don't want to stay _the_ victim. Predators have the edge in confidence, among other things. It is important to take that edge away. A primary concept in the F.I.G.H.T. program is to turn from a victim into a predator by countering violence with far more violence thereby putting your attacker in a victim's mindset. The techniques are designed to do that by using aggressiveness and quick response.

The F.I.G.H.T. program mindset is like an old adage that states, "keep your friends close and your enemies closer." Once an engagement begins (except at the very outset of a knife attack) you want to bring your adversary into you or step into him. This is the key to switching from victim to predator. By 'smothering' him, we greatly limit his ability to counterattack. Sometimes in the process we will 'pin' or 'plug' part of him to us or to himself, for example pinning one of his arms to (against) him during certain strikes. By this we mean securing that body part to his body or our body in such a way that it is rendered ineffective- it is taken out of the fight.

Generally, when we attempt to control any part of our attacker's body, we do so using multiple points of contact. For example, if we want to control his arm, we do not grasp it with one hand only. We might use both hands, or we might use one hand and secure his arm against his or our body- either way there are two points of contact which makes our grip much more secure. Also, whenever we are using our hands or arms to secure our attacker, we will generally mean to secure him with one arm or hand over the target body part and one under. Sometimes we refer to this as the battery concept (batteries have opposite poles). **Pictures 1 and 2** are good examples of this. It is a much more secure hold than if both of your grips were facing in the same direction. When our attacker puts his hands on us, we are _grateful!_ By doing this he is telling us what he is about to do _and_ he is demonstrat-

Mindset and Principles

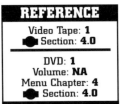

REFERENCE

Video Tape: **1**
Section: **4.0**

DVD: **1**
Volume: **NA**
Menu Chapter: **4**
Section: **4.0**

**F.I.G.H.T. Tip:
BREAHTING**

*You must program
yourself to breath while
fighting. The simplest
way to do so is to
breath out through your
mouth each time you
practice and strike. In a
live class, you will
typically hear sounds
like "shhh" or "ushh".
This is forced breathing
out. You will automati-
cally breath in.
Always breath.*

**F.I.G.H.T. Tip:
SHORT CIRCUIT**

*We use pain to short
circuit our attacker's
thought process. The
frequency of your
attacks is key to
creating a short
circuit effect.*

ing that he has not yet deployed a weapon. We think 'Thank you for the gift'. And, we keep that gift. Most of our techniques will have you pin his hands to you if he touches you to eliminate his ability to deploy a weapon or to change his attack. In some systems, the focus is disconnecting. Unless you can immediately and safely escape with no chance the attacker can catch you (or shoot or stab you-you don't know if he's armed), it is generally a mistake to disconnect once you are con-nected. Destruction is usually the correct choice.

A fight is very stressful and will drain your energy very quickly. Each of us has a unique reserve of ener-gy. You do not know who has a greater capacity for exertion under stress. Therefore, you want to work as little as possible and simultaneously have the greatest possible benefit. In this way, you will deplete your reserves slowly. Once you are exhausted (no more gas in the tank), your attacker better be completely out of the fight or you are in trouble. To make this happen, each technique needs to be executed with straight-line (shortest distance = least unnecessary) motion and on target (or 'tight') motions. To do this, you must develop smooth, technically accurate (=effective) techniques versus overly focusing on developing speed. In the F.I.G.H.T. program, 'smooth is fast'. Most importantly, to make sure that you do not waste any energy without an immediate benefit, every motion should damage your attacker. Every time you touch your attacker he should feel pain. For example, when a technique requires you to position part of your body against an attacker's body we might say 'bump' or 'jilt' him in the process. Pain accumulates and each of us can only tol-erate so much. By inflicting damage with each motion, every time your energy reserve is used so is his.

Creating pain has another effect. When the brain is processing pain its focus goes to the source of the pain. This keeps it momentarily distracted and focuses its attention where you want it. Every time you damage your attacker, you are also momentarily controlling his thought process. You will win the fight when you 'over-whelm him' and he runs out of gas, loses his will to fight, or is physically incapable of normal body func-tioning. You do this by creating damage with every technique and 'overlapping' those techniques – execut-ing them one after the other immediately so that his brain keeps getting directed to different pain sources without enough time to decide what might happen next and develop a counterattack or defense.

In developing strategies for you to use, the F.I.G.H.T. program recognizes another important principle of

how the brain functions. Essentially, your brain finds it easier to deal with stimuli and organize cohesive thoughts and reactions to them if they are happening in the same region of your body. For our purposes, we divide the attacker's body into three zones – high, mid-dle and low. When we designed the street attacks and other counterattacks they generally follow high strike with low or vice versa. This makes it even more diffi-cult for your attacker's brain to formulate a defense against you because the pain you are causing moves from zone to zone. If you have to improvise, it is a good idea to follow strikes in one zone with strikes in another to keep your attacker's brain confused. Knowing the distracting effect of pain, you can impro-vise if things are not going the way they are laid out in the book. In many systems, they present a series of strikes as though they are guaranteed to work pre-cisely. Our street attacks work. However, every person has different capabilities and reactions to a fight. Use pain if things are not going smoothly. If a person does not loosen up when the technique says he needs to, HIT HIM AGAIN! It is rarely a mistake to add additional strikes if you feel you need to in a real fight. Go with your gut.

Virtually all blocks in the system are referred to as 90 degree blocks. This is the action of blocking with the forearm while the arm is bent 90 degrees at the elbow. This is essential to creating the strongest possible block. For example, if a person is trying to hit you with a stick and you are forced by the timing to block, if you block his swinging arm with your forearm while bent 90 degrees, the block will be solid and likely stop his motion. If your arm is extended more than 90 degrees, his arm will slide down your arm into you. Likewise, if your arm is bent less than 90 degrees, your block will likely collapse and his motion into you will continue. Ninety degree blocks can be executed in many direc-tions to defend against many angles of attack. Having said this, the Haganah system rarely relies on block-ing. Therefore your training in 90 degree blocks will be limited to those techniques which use it and this train-ing will help you develop proper blocking techniques in case you act in accordance with your personal instinct to block in a specific situation.

TARGETS

The Haganah system is designed to enable you to attack the weakest parts of an attacker's body in the most effective way possible. While you can never assume that you know an attacker's capability, the one thing you do know is that your attacker is human. All human bodies have strong points, such as bone, and

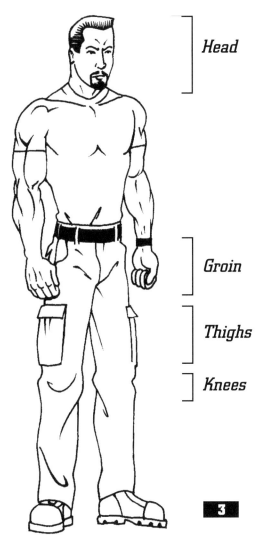

Head

Groin

Thighs

Knees

3

niques, you can control his body. Where the head goes, the body follows. The connection of the head to the spinal column is fragile and as a last resort in a life threatening situation may be snapped using Haganah techniques, resulting in the attacker's death. Striking the eyes with the fingers will blur vision or distract the individual. Striking the ears with cupped hands will disrupt a person's equilibrium and distract them. Striking below the ear and behind the jaw will also disrupt a person's equilibrium. Striking the nose properly is likely to be painful and cause profuse bleeding. Just below the nose, where the upper jaw meets the base of the nose there are many nerves. In certain techniques, extreme pressure will be applied there causing great pain. Striking or otherwise putting pressure on the throat at the Adam's apple will cause gagging and intense pain. Striking the side of the throat at or near the carotid artery can cause momentary loss of consciousness or distract or shock the individual.

weak points, such as organs or nerves. It is important that you develop the skills to hit the weak points, the mindset to be willing to hit them and an understanding of the most likely general effects of hitting them (no two people will respond precisely the same way to a given strike). The targets that we will typically hit or otherwise use to control an attack are shown in **Pictures 3** (front) **and 4** (back) and are:

Head
- Eyes - Ears - Nose - Throat
- Upper lip joint with Nose
- Area below the ear - (Triangle) **Picture 3A**
Hands
- Back of Hands - Fingers

Backbone (spinal column)
Groin
Thighs
Knees
Ankles

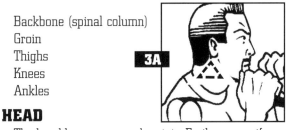

3A

HEAD

The head has many weak points. Furthermore, if you can control a person's head, as you will see in the tech-

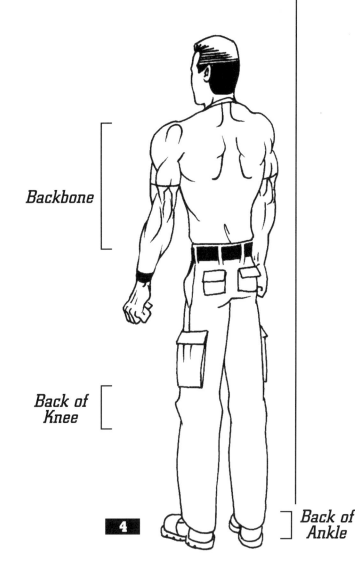

Backbone

Back of
Knee

Back of
Ankle

4

REFERENCE

Video Tape: **1**
◆ Section: **7.0**

DVD: **1**
Volume: **NA**
Menu Chapter: **7**
◆ Section: **7.0**

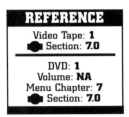

GROIN

The groin is a sensitive area on both men and women. Attacked properly, it <u>likely</u> will at least momentarily incapacitate your attacker and if they are standing cause them to bend forward and possibly reach for their groin area.

HANDS

The backs of the hands are very sensitive. Striking them properly will cause pain and will cause the attacker to loosen his grip. The fingers are easily controlled or broken- both painful.

BACKBONE (SPINAL COLUMN)

The backbone is easily broken if struck properly. Breaking it will at a minimum cause paralysis and shock. It might cause death.

THIGHS

The thighs can be struck to cause a 'Charlie horse' or deadening of the leg momentarily. It is painful and can cause a person to loose their balance. The thigh bone (femur) can also be broken with a well placed kick.

KNEES

The knees are easily damaged which may create a relatively permanent incapacitation.

ANKLES

The ankles are easily snapped and broken, incapacitating an attacker. It is virtually impossible to walk with a broken ankle.

The F.I.G.H.T. program is not about sport fighting. Nor is it about two evenly matched opponents 'duking it out'. It is about someone whose skills and intent are unknown to you violently attacking you. It is about situations where it is you or him. Perhaps he is bigger, or stronger, or armed. Perhaps there are several assailants. There are no rules in such a situation except to survive. To do so you must attack weaknesses. Fast. Hard. Overwhelmingly. Your only consideration is whether deadly force or permanent incapacitation is required. Do not kill unless you reasonably believe your life is threatened. You will have to justify deadly force. Attack until your attacker is incapable of attacking back or until you can safely escape. All other civilized behavior is 'out the window'.

WEAPONS

You have many weapons to work with in the Haganah system: head, hands, elbows, knees, shins, feet and teeth (as brutal as that sounds). Your head can be used for a 'head butt'- typically slamming the opponent's nose into the top of your head. Your hands can be used to strike as regular fists, hammer fists, and palm strikes or to grab, secure or break parts of your attacker's body. Fingers can be used to jab or gouge the eyes or throat. Your elbows are bone and therefore very hard, so they can be used to hit your attacker very effectively. Likewise, your knees are driven by the strongest muscles in your body and are bone also. They can cause substantial damage if used effectively. Your shins and feet can be used in kicks to inflict damage. And finally, when necessary, you can bite. Remember, violence can only be defeated with more violence, overwhelming violence and perfect intention to survive. Desperate situations call for desperate measures. When all else fails – you can bite. The only rule- make sure your teeth meet. Bite all the way through.

PROPER TECHNIQUES

FISTS

A proper fist is shown in **Picture 5**. Note that the wrist is straight and the hand is squeezed tightly. If you hit someone with a loose fist, you may fracture your hand. If you do so with a bent wrist, you may break your wrist. In either case, you will be at a significant and possibly decisive disadvantage. Although simple, making and maintaining a proper fist is essential. The fist can be used to strike head on with the knuckles as shown in **Picture 6** or as a 'hammer fist' with the side of the hand as shown in **Picture 7**.

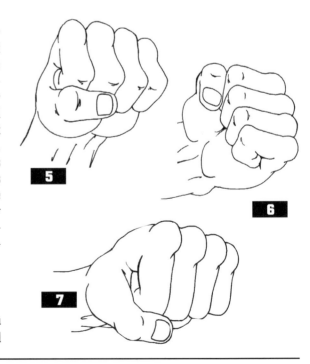

STANCES

As previously discussed, the F.I.G.H.T. series is based upon the integrated Israeli fighting system, Haganah.

Haganah has three stances from which all fighting (other than initial self defense) occur: a hand-to-hand combat fighting stance, a tactical knife fighting stance and a combat shooting stance. We will also reference a self defense or neutral stance or posture, but this is not a specifically designed stance. It refers to you in a neutral posture, either standing normally, with your hands at your sides, sitting down or lying down. We will only cover a standing self defense posture in this series. The seated and lying down self-defense postures are covered in advanced tapes, as are the tactical knife fighting and shooting stances.

FIGHTING STANCE

The fighting stance is **Pictured in 8 and 9.** Your feet are about shoulder width apart. Your left leg is forward and your right is back (opposite if left-handed), with your rear heel up. Your knees are slightly bent and your weight is evenly distributed. Your hands are up such that if you stick your thumbs out they should touch your cheeks. You are relaxed and your hands are open. If you punch you will close your hands into tight fists. When confronted by an attacker, if at all possible, assume a fighting stance as in **Picture**

10. If you turn your hands out and keep them open you may appear as though you are trying to avoid, rather than participate, in a fight. This may serve to reduce tensions and avoid the encounter altogether. From a legal perspective, witnesses may say that you appeared to try to diffuse rather than escalate the situation. This perception will be both accurate and legally helpful to you. If possible, leave and avoid the fight. If not, you are properly positioned to counterattack or preemptively attack if necessary. Remember, if your first strike is a punch, to close your hands as you begin to throw the punch.

PRACTICE

The key to becoming "programmed" is proper repetition. Programming is embedding the individual moves and strikes and the sequence for each attack into your muscle memory so that at the necessary time you perform effectively almost without thinking. You must practice each individual strike, kick, grab, slap, etc **repeatedly with correct form** to enable each one to be automatically replayed by your neuro-muscular system. It is like a baseball player swinging a bat. The best ones swing properly nearly all the time because they have swung properly so many times before. There is nothing magic here. It is not enough just to practice the parts. You have to practice full attacks over and over **with correct form**. For this you will need a partner.

To effectively practice with correct form, you must practice the elements slowly and smoothly, not fast. Smooth is fast. Fast is not necessarily smooth. Build smoothness into your moves and speed will come.

As with any serious training program, you should practice at least three days per week with each session lasting at least 45 minutes. Of course the more frequent and focused your practice sessions are the better your results will be. Also, remember to warm-up and stretch at the start of each practice session.

REFERENCE
Video Tape: **1**
◆ Section: **5.0**
DVD: **1**
Volume: **NA**
Menu Chapter: **5**
◆ Section: **5.0**

Proper Techniques

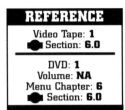

REFERENCE

Video Tape: **1**
◀█ Section: **6.0**

DVD: **1**
Volume: **NA**
Menu Chapter: **6**
◀█ Section: **6.0**

This manual is keyed to the videos (or DVDs). If you have them, view the appropriate part at the outset of your practice. This is extremely helpful. Once you feel comfortable with the strikes, you need not keep viewing them on the tapes. However, you should always view the more advanced street scenarios or knife defenses and gun disarms you are about to practice before you do so. This will help you to more rapidly increase your skill level.

You should then practice each punch, kick, knee, and other strikes at least 5 times on each side as a warm-up. Then, with a partner, you should practice a street attack, gun disarm, or knife defense until you are comfortable with it.

When practicing with a partner, it is best for you both to be learning the system. It is essential to move slowly, wear appropriate protective gear, particularly groin cups, and not to strike with any force. You need only touch with a light impact to train your body to hit the target properly. **DO NOT PRACTICE ANY LETHAL OR INCAPACITATING TECHNIQUE ON ANOTHER PERSON. It is sufficient merely to get to the position from which you would execute such a technique and to study the balance of the technique, as described in this manual and very effectively depicted on the DVDs/tapes.** For more in-depth instruction and advanced training, these techniques are taught in person at our seminars. and Authorized Centers. For more information, see our website at *www.fight2survive.com.*

If you have prior martial arts experience, you are used to the concept of repeatedly practicing sequences of moves and building up to a complete attack. For the benefit of those of you with no such prior experience, it is a good idea when practicing a complete scenario with a partner, to practice only the entry (first move or two) 7 times. Then build up, adding the counterattack (next few components), and the finishing technique (the final moves). Practice each segment 7 times. Then practice it start to finish 7 times. Then practice it 7 more times increasing your speed (but only as fast as you can while maintaining complete and smooth control). Have your partner do the same. It helps you learn if you observe each other's mistakes and identify them. After you have both practiced your sets of 7, practice give-and-take - you do it once then they do it once, alternating back and forth. **ALWAYS USE CAUTION AND WEAR PROTECTIVE GEAR.**

If you do this at least three times per week, in under three months you will have completed one complete rotation through the techniques and have likely practiced many of the moves between 500 and 1000 times. Then keep repeating and add-in additional IDFS advanced techniques to become even more proficient. It all adds up. If you then look back, you will see that you have developed potent self-defense skills. If in the process you choose to invest in attending our seminar series or Authorized Centers, you can reach a high level of skill in a short period of time.

FUNDAMENTAL STRIKES

The fundamental strikes that dominate the F.I.G.H.T. program are also the primary tactics employed in the Haganah system. Variations of these strikes are used in different ways in the system and in the self-defense techniques you will learn in this F.I.G.H.T. program. By practicing the group of strikes which follow without variation you will be well prepared to apply them or variations of them effectively. It is important to understand that the specific strikes described here are what we have determined to be the best set of strikes to build your capability quickly and to incorporate all the concepts of the system. As you begin to learn specific attack scenarios and thereafter as you begin to have to improvise against new attacks, you will use variations on the skill set created by these strikes.

The fundamental strikes are divided into two groups, fighting stance techniques and neutral (self-defense) stance techniques. Neutral stance techniques are typically used when a person attacks with little or no warning and you are caught off guard. Fighting stance techniques are used when the situation allows you time to prepare for the attack or when a self-defense situation becomes a fight.

All of the following techniques are typically used from a fighting stance, so get into a fighting stance while practicing. Practice each technique in your primary lead (left if right-handed, right if left-handed) and then also practice in the opposite lead because you may not be able to choose your primary lead at various points during a fight.

FRONT HAND TECHNIQUES

Front hand techniques use your front hand to strike your attacker. All are used to inflict damage; however, they each have one of three primary characteristics - intercepting, setting-up, or repelling your attacker. This does not mean that they only cause the primary characteristic to occur, but rather that they are naturally most effective at that goal. An intercepting technique is used to stop your attacker in the spot where he is standing. A setting-up technique is used to distract your attacker prior to your second strike. A repelling technique is used to cause your attacker to be thrust backward.

With front hand techniques, speed is more important than power. You will use these techniques as a first or second step in a series of devastating strikes designed to overwhelm your attacker.

STRAIGHT PUNCH

Primary Characteristic- Intercepting
Target- Anywhere from Solar plexus to nose

1. Begin in fighting stance. **Picture 11**

2. Rapidly extend front hand while keeping fist vertical. Make sure you fully extend your hand and you tighten your fist. **Picture 12**

3. Simultaneously rotate your body from the hips, driving the punch. The power in the punch comes from strong hip rotation. **Picture 12**

4. At the completion of extending your hand, your arm should snap back to its starting position and your hips should simultaneously rotate back to their starting position.

REFERENCE

Video Tape: **1**
Section: **8.0**

DVD: **1**
Volume: **NA**
Menu Chapter: **8**
Section: **8.0**

F.I.G.H.T. Tip:
Weapon Moves First
In each hand strike your weapon (hand) moves first and is given more force by the rotation of your body.

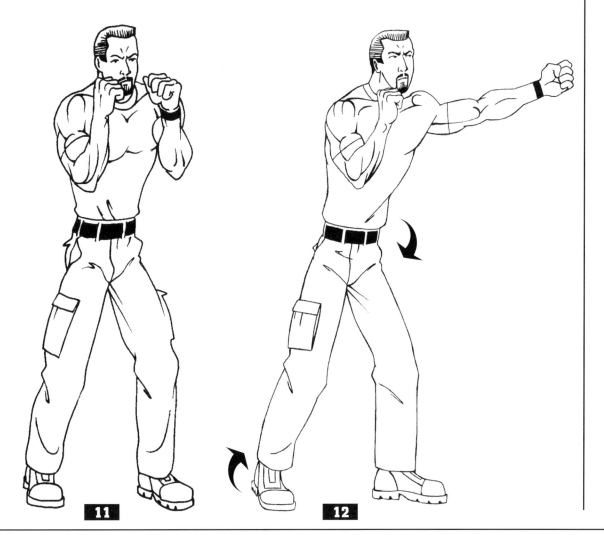

11

12

REFERENCE

Video Tape: **1**
◆ Section: **9.0**

DVD: **1**
Volume: **NA**
Menu Chapter: **9**
◆ Section: **9.0**

**F.I.G.H.T. Tip:
Brushing Eyes**

*The finger jab does
not need to poke into
the eyes. You will still
momentarily disrupt
your attacker's vision
even if you only flick
your fingers into the
eye area.*

FINGER JAB

Primary Characteristic - Set up
Target - Eyes

1. Begin in fighting stance. **Picture 13**

2. This technique has the same mechanics as the straight punch.

3. Rapidly extend front hand keeping your fingers extended and together but not in a fist. Keep your wrist loose. **Picture 14**. Make sure you fully extend your hand and you flick your fingers into the attacker's eyes. Ideally, your hand will be tilted about 45 degrees. **Picture 15**

4. Simultaneously rotate your body from the hips, increasing the jab's reach. **Picture 15**

5. At the completion of extending your hand, your arm should snap back to its starting position and your hips should simultaneously rotate back to their starting position.

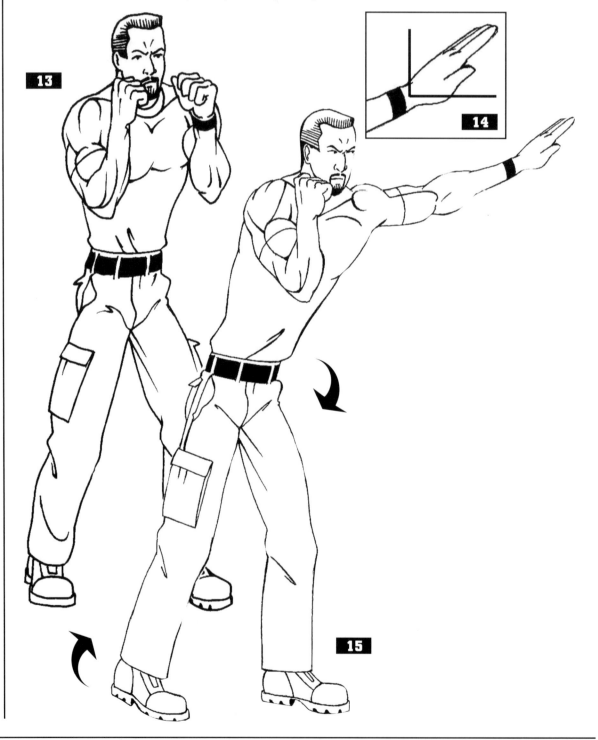

THROAT STRIKE

Primary Characteristic - Repelling
Target - Throat - Adam's Apple

1. Begin in fighting stance. **Picture. 16**

2. This technique has the same mechanics as the straight punch and finger jab.

3. Rapidly extend front hand keeping your fingers extended and thumb out about 90 degrees as though you are about to grab a large can. **Picture 17**.

Make sure you fully extend your hand and strike the Adams apple coming up from underneath. **Picture 18**

4. Simultaneously rotate your body from the hips, driving the strike. The strike's power and effectiveness comes from strong hip rotation. **Picture 18**

5. At the completion of extending your hand, your arm should snap back to its starting position and your hips should simultaneously rotate back to their starting position.

REFERENCE
Video Tape: **1**
◆ Section: **10.0**
DVD: **1**
Volume: **NA**
Menu Chapter: **10**
◆ Section: **10.0**

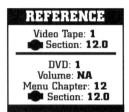

REFERENCE

Video Tape: **1**
Section: **12.0**

DVD: **1**
Volume: **NA**
Menu Chapter: **12**
Section: **12.0**

Like they sound, rear hand techniques use your rear hand to strike your attacker. You can develop more power with your rear hand than your front because in a fighting stance your dominant hand is in the rear, more of your body weight will be behind the hand when you rotate and in some cases you will be moving into the punch/strike.

These techniques are designed to inflict pain, cause psychological and physical damage, and 'loosen up' your attacker for you to achieve a dominant position.

PALM STRIKE
Target(s) – Nose (chin)

1. Begin in fighting stance. **Picture 19**

2. This technique will typically be used in response to an attacker attempting to strike you with an object from above. **Picture 20**

3. Consistent with your instincts, raise your front arm above your head. Bend the elbow 90 degrees to <u>firmly</u> project against the attack and crouch down. **Picture 21**

4. After covering and crouching down, use your body like a spring and drive upward with your rear hand extending to strike the attacker's nose or chin from underneath with the base of your palm. **Picture 22** The upward motion of your body adds power to the strike.

5. Since attackers trying to hit you with objects tend to strike repeatedly, do not rotate your body and blocking arm and thereby move your protecting arm from above your head. Practice this in front of a mirror and you will see that, if you rotate during the palm heel strike your head becomes exposed.

6. At the completion of the strike, your arms should snap back to their starting position.

UP AND OVER

Target- Lower ribs just behind the attacker's elbow.

1. Begin in fighting stance. **Picture 23**

2. This technique will typically be used in clinch range similar to **Picture 24**.

3. Drop your rear hand and lower your body slightly.

4. Ideally, the punch comes up from beneath and strikes behind your attacker's front elbow, continuing "up and over" to his opposite side shoulder. It is important to pivot on your rear foot while rotating and driving the punch into your attacker's rib cage. Keep your wrist locked and your arm at a 90 degree bend. The practice punch is over when your hand is in front of your face. In reality, your punch should dig into your attacker's short lower ribs, where there is no muscle protection, causing pain and damage. **Picture 25**

5. At the completion of the strike, your arms should snap back to their starting position.

REFERENCE

Video Tape: **1**
Section: **13.0**

DVD: **1**
Volume: **NA**
Menu Chapter: **13**
Section: **13.0**

F.I.G.H.T. Note:
Picture 24
Illustration
Picture 24 is merely used to illustrate the relative position of the two opponents, i.e., their close proximity.

23

24

25

Rear Hand Techniques - Cross

REFERENCE
Video Tape: **1**
Section: **11.0**

DVD: **1**
Volume: **NA**
Menu Chapter: **11**
Section: **11.0**

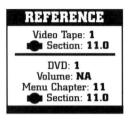

CROSS

Target- Typically between the nose and the solar plexus

1. Begin in fighting stance. **Picture 26**

2. Step toward your attacker while pushing off and moving forward with your rear foot. If you only move your front leg, your body will lower which will make you strike lower on your attacker, rendering the punch ineffective.

3. At the same time as your rear leg completes its forward motion, rotate strongly into a forward punch with your rear hand. Make sure to fully extend your arm and that your rear foot rotates with your hips. This is your most powerful punch. **Picture 27**

4. At the completion of the strike, your arms should snap back to their starting position.

5. As with every technique you practice, you end up back in fighting stance.

**F.I.G.H.T. Tip:
Building Defense**
The cross should end with your hand at full extension directly in front of your face, not to either side. This position builds a defensive element into this technique.

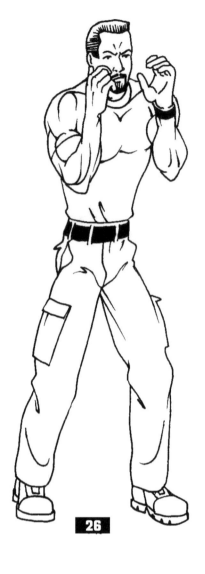

26

27

EYE GOUGE
Target- eyes

1. You can execute an eye gouge from many positions.

2. Grab your attacker's head with your thumbs positioned on his eyes. Ideally, your thumbs should point toward each other separated only by the nose. **Picture 28**

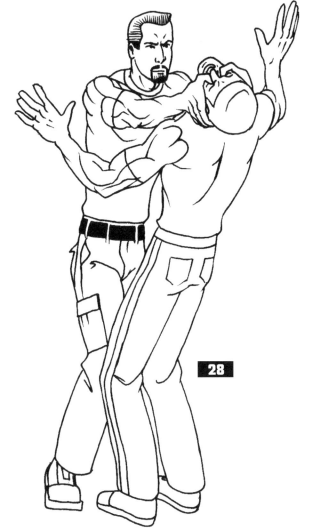

28

3. Dig your thumbs into his eyes. Assess the situation; in a life or death struggle, dig deeply — getting behind the eyes and dislodging them. Otherwise, simply press hard- creating severe pain, disrupting his vision, and causing him to panic. **Picture 29**

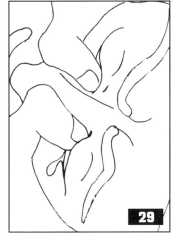

29

EAR SMASH
Target- ears

1. You can execute an ear smash from many positions.

2. Cup your hands. **Picture 30**

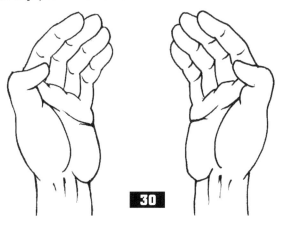

30

3. Keep your hands cupped and thrust them forward at about shoulder width apart with your attacker's head centered between them. Forcefully bring your hands together by smashing over your attacker's ears. **Picture 31**

4. When thrusting forward, do not open your arms too wide, as it gives your attacker an opportunity to block or otherwise defeat your attack.

5. A properly executed ear smash will disrupt your attacker's equilibrium and distract him by creating pain and ringing in his ears.

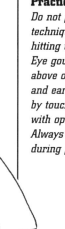

31

REFERENCE

Video Tape: **1**
Section: **28.0**

DVD: **1**
Volume: **NA**
Menu Chapter: **28**
Section: **28.0**

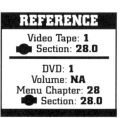

F.I.G.H.T. Tip:
Practice Safety
Do not practice these techniques by actually hitting the target areas. Eye gouge your partner above or below the eyes and ear smash them by touching the head with open fingers. Always use caution during practice.

Other Hand Techniques - Groin Strike and Knock Knock

REFERENCE
Video Tape: **1**
◆ Section: **28.0**

DVD: **1**
Volume: **NA**
Menu Chapter: **28**
◆ Section: **28.0**

Fight Tip:
Head Butts
A head butt can also prove tactically effective. The F.I.G.H.T. system utilizes a slightly different style of head butt, ensuring the safety of your forehead.

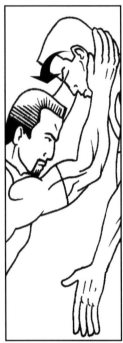

To execute this, drop base and pull the face down into the top of your head. This avoids bone on bone contact, which should only be risked if headbutting backwards into the face if an attacker is behind you.

GROIN STRIKE

Target- Groin- from underneath

1. You can execute a groin strike from many positions.

2. In most cases, you will be slapping rather than punching the groin. It is usually more effective, unless you are on the ground. (Ground fighting will be covered in a separate manual and set of videos. For more information, go to *www.fight2survive.com*).

3. You can slap the groin with the front or back of your hand, whichever feels more natural to you depending on your position. **Picture 32**

4. The most important element is to flick your wrist and slap from underneath. This will allow you to penetrate clothing and if fighting a male will maximize the likelihood of striking the testicles (which will cause the most pain).

5. A properly executed groin strike will usually cause your attacker to bend at the waist and/or reach for his groin.

KNOCK KNOCK

Target- Back of hands

1. This is designed to cause an attacker to open his hands.

2. When an attacker has a "bear hug" type hold on your body that leaves your hands free, you can strike the back of his hands as shown in **Picture 33** to cause him to open them. Depending upon the desired effect (letting go completely or just opening up) you can strike as many times as is necessary.

3. The important thing is to keep your wrist loose and strike fast and hard with the <u>knuckles</u> of your first finger joint. **Picture 34**

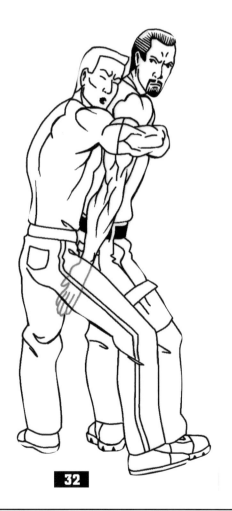

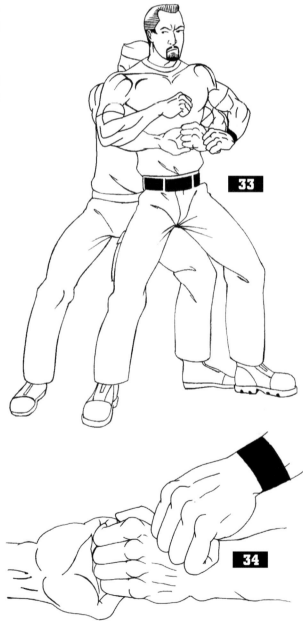

Elbows are very effective weapons. The elbow is a bone, and consequently is very hard. There is no need to clench your fist when hitting with the elbow. In fact, if you do, you will be fighting against the motion of the elbow thereby slowing it down. Elbows are up-close weapons, so typically they are either your last line of defense in a self-defense initial engagement, or are used in clinch range in a fight. We will cover fighting elbows here.

OVERHEAD ELBOW
Primary Characteristic
Target- Forehead

1. Begin in fighting stance. **Picture 35**

2. Step forward while pushing off your rear leg and then sliding it forward. Both legs move. If you only move your front leg, your body will lower which will make you strike lower on your attacker, rendering the elbow less effective.

3. Simultaneously, place your front hand on the top of your forehead as shown in **Picture 36**. This is to protect against your attacker elbowing you.

4. The elbow is thrown by essentially swimming into the armpit of your front hand with the rear hand as shown in **Picture 37 and 38**, while rotating the hips and pivoting the rear foot. This movement should be executed tight and fast. The objective is to graze the attacker's forehead with the tip of your elbow either cutting it open or causing a lump. Speed is more important than power, and the pivot of the rear leg will provide both.

5. At the completion of the strike, your arms should snap back to their starting position.

6. As with every technique you practice, you end up back in fighting stance.

REFERENCE
Video Tape: **1**
Section: **17.0**

DVD: **1**
Volume: **NA**
Menu Chapter: **17**
Section: **17.0**

REFERENCE
Video Tape: **1**
Section: **24.0**

DVD: **1**
Volume: **NA**
Menu Chapter: **24**
Section: **24.0**

F.I.G.H.T. Tip: Positioning
When techniques include "stepping in" it is because of the assumed relative position between you and your opponent. If they are appropriate in a situation where a forward step is not required, they can still be used effectively.

35 36 37 38

REFERENCE
Video Tape: **1**
◆ Section: **25.0**

DVD: **1**
Volume: **NA**
Menu Chapter: **25**
◆ Section: **25.0**

FRONT ELBOW

Target- Throat or Head

1. Begin in fighting stance. **Picture 39**

2. As with the overhead elbow, your other hand should be placed on your forehead to protect against your attacker elbowing you. **Picture 40**

3. Swing your front elbow in an arc level with your shoulder towards your rear shoulder. **Picture 41**

4. Simultaneously shift your weight towards the rear, dropping your rear heel and pivoting your front foot to allow the elbow more rotation.

5. This is a quick snap of the elbow. Build speed. Also, both shifting your weight and pivoting your front foot are critical to developing adequate power and speed behind the elbow. Focus on pivoting properly during practice.

6. At the completion of the strike, your arms should snap back to their starting position.

7. As with every fighting technique you practice, you end up back in fighting stance.

SENSOR ELBOW

Primary Characteristic – Defensive
Target- none

1. The sensor elbow involves no footwork and is intended to follow your natural reaction of covering up when surprised. We will practice it in fighting stance.

2. **Picture 42**

3. Raise your front arm as shown in **Picture 43** so that the crook of your elbow is centered on your face. You should see your bicep in front of your face. Do not step forward.

4. Simultaneously turtle up as shown in **Picture 44**. Bring your shoulder up and tighten up like a turtle in its shell.

5. This elbow will be used as your defense when your attacker has moved too quickly for you to do anything else. It's instinctive. It will be followed by an attack as soon as you feel contact on your arm.

6. This position will cause a punch to either hit your elbow, which will damage your attacker's hand, or be deflected left or right.

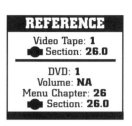

REFERENCE

Video Tape: **1**
◆ Section: **26.0**

DVD: **1**
Volume: **NA**
Menu Chapter: **26**
◆ Section: **26.0**

F.I.G.H.T. Tip:
Elbow Combination
This elbow can be effectively combined with the Overhead Elbow. Practice using this elbow standing in place as though you deflected a surprise punch and then step forward while transitioning to an Overhead Elbow.

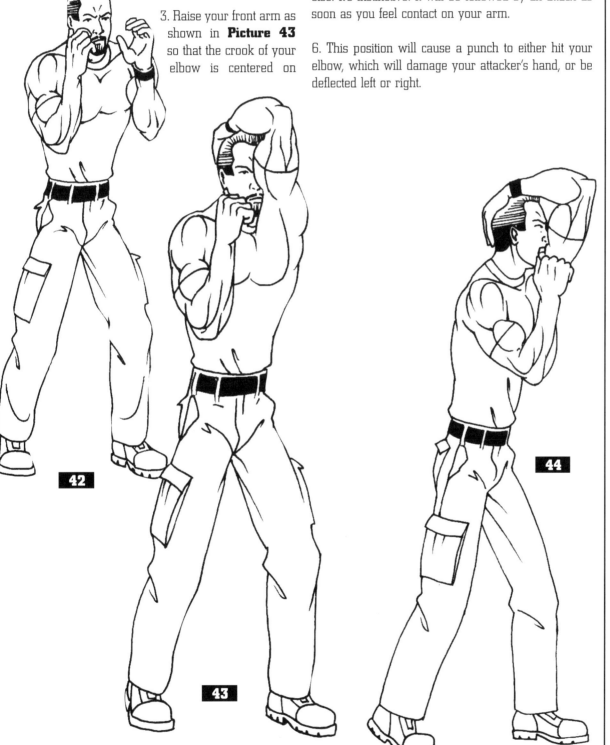

42

43

44

REFERENCE

Video Tape: **1**
◆ Section: **27.0**

DVD: **1**
Volume: **NA**
Menu Chapter: **27**
◆ Section: **27.0**

Knees are very effective weapons in clinch range. We will practice one knee from fighting stance to get the mechanics down, however the system focuses on using knees against low-line targets- that is targets at waist level (low abdomen) or below (groin, thighs), or any body part that has been forced down below waist level -such as the head in certain techniques. All knee strikes have the same basic mechanics as the knee to the groin described below. The proper method of delivery is to hit with the knee bone, not the thigh.

KNEE TO THE GROIN (LOW LINE KNEE)

1. Begin in fighting stance. **Picture 45**

2. Knee with your rear leg while clearing both hands to the same side you knee from. Simultaneously lean back. **Picture 46**

3. The objective is to come up underneath the groin hard.

4. It is important to note the following:

   a. By having the knee driven by the back leg you gain far more power than if both legs were side by side. This is an important concept. When the leg is back prior to kneeing, we refer to it as 'loaded up'. **Picture 47**

   b. By clearing both hands to the side you help maintain your balance and mimic certain techniques which will be taught later

   c. By leaning back while you knee, you add power, help maintain your balance and, most importantly, remove your head from your attacker's hitting or cutting range.

5. After delivering the knee, snap back to fighting stance.

6. By practicing this knee repeatedly on both sides, you will develop strong kneeing ability for all types of knee strikes.

Kicks will be practiced from a fighting stance. There are three basic kicks in the system: round kick, front kick and side kick. Kicks can be delivered from either a left lead (left leg in front), or a right lead (right leg in front), but should be practiced both ways as you may not be able to choose your lead in a given situation.

ROUND KICK
Target- Thigh

1. Begin in fighting stance, left lead. **Picture 48**

2. The kick is delivered with the rear leg in an arcing (semi-circular) or swinging motion that rises up and **chops down** at the thigh. See **Picture 49**. The leg is used almost like a club, although the knee can be bent and used to add power with a snap at the end. The kick should be delivered with force as though you are striking through your opponent's leg. Ideally, you are striking his thigh with your lower shin. Do not strike with the foot. The shin is bone and is very painful when used in this fashion.

3. Simultaneously with the swinging of the leg, the upper body should lean back in the opposite direction, the front foot should pivot (it helps to rise up on the ball of your foot), and the now leading hand should be swung towards the back. See **Picture 49**. These motions have the following effects:

a. The bending will help you keep your balance, particularly if you miss, and will help keep your throat out of reach of a knife.

b. The pivot will allow the leg to swing with maximum power.

c. The opposing swing of the arm will also help you remain balanced.

4. Upon completion of the kick, return to fighting stance.

5. This kick should be practiced from both left and right leads.

REFERENCE
Video Tape: **1**
Section: **29.0**

DVD: **1**
Volume: **NA**
Menu Chapter: **29**
Section: **29.0**

**F.I.G.H.T. Tip:
Effectiveness**
If you draw a diagonal line from the middle of the opponent's targeted thigh to his opposite leg's knee and deliver the round kick along that line you will "chop down" properly.

48

49

REFERENCE

Video Tape: **1**
Section: **30.0**

DVD: **1**
Volume: **NA**
Menu Chapter: **30**
Section: **30.0**

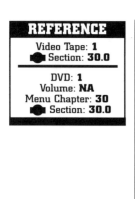

FRONT KICK

Target- Groin, smashing the testicles into the pelvis bone

1. Begin in fighting stance, left lead. **Picture 50**

2. The kick is delivered with the rear leg coming up underneath the groin. You are not aiming for the groin, rather you are forcefully and quickly bring you leg up between your attackers legs, striking the groin with anywhere from your instep to your shin. **Picture 51**

3. While you are delivering the kick, bend backwards to maintain balance, clear away from a possible knife slash (which we assume is present) or a punch, and add power. Simultaneously, drop your hand on your kicking side to add to balance. **Picture 51**.

4. Upon completion of the kick, return to fighting stance.

5. This kick should be practiced from both left and right leads.

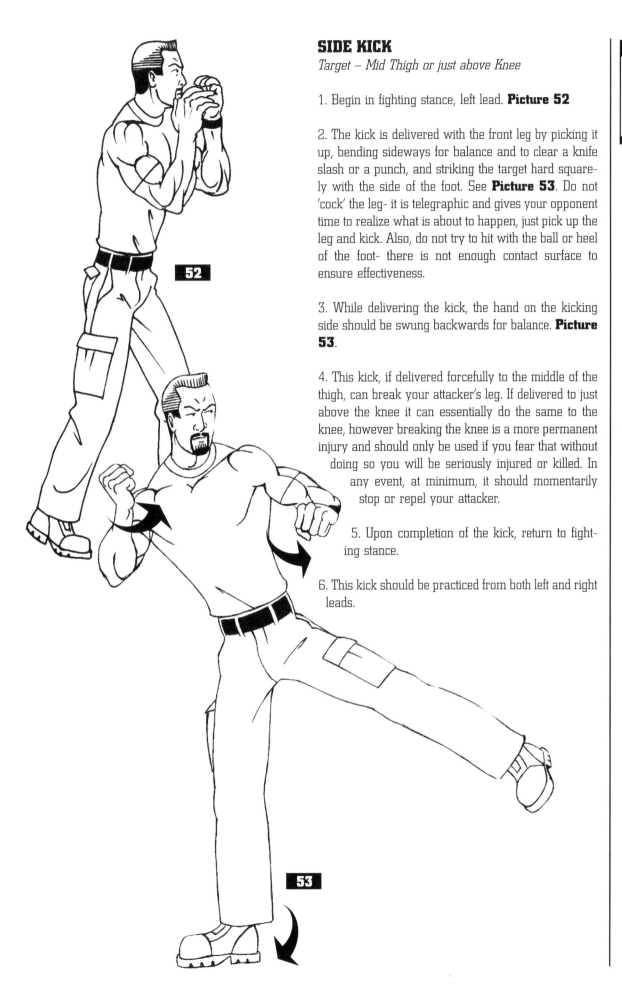

SIDE KICK

Target – Mid Thigh or just above Knee

1. Begin in fighting stance, left lead. **Picture 52**

2. The kick is delivered with the front leg by picking it up, bending sideways for balance and to clear a knife slash or a punch, and striking the target hard squarely with the side of the foot. See **Picture 53**. Do not 'cock' the leg- it is telegraphic and gives your opponent time to realize what is about to happen, just pick up the leg and kick. Also, do not try to hit with the ball or heel of the foot- there is not enough contact surface to ensure effectiveness.

3. While delivering the kick, the hand on the kicking side should be swung backwards for balance. **Picture 53**.

4. This kick, if delivered forcefully to the middle of the thigh, can break your attacker's leg. If delivered to just above the knee it can essentially do the same to the knee, however breaking the knee is a more permanent injury and should only be used if you fear that without doing so you will be seriously injured or killed. In any event, at minimum, it should momentarily stop or repel your attacker.

5. Upon completion of the kick, return to fighting stance.

6. This kick should be practiced from both left and right leads.

REFERENCE

Video Tape: **1**
● Section: **31.0**

DVD: **1**
Volume: **NA**
Menu Chapter: **31**
● Section: **31.0**

F.I.G.H.T. Tip:
Gross Motor Skills
Do not try to execute kicks with the tip of your foot (groin kick) or ball or heel of your foot (side kick). Hitting effectively with less than the full foot for a side kick or shin for groin kick is a fine motor skill. Fine motor skills degrade under stress.

F.I.G.H.T. Principles And Combatives

Self-Defense (Neutral) Stance Techniques

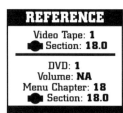

REFERENCE
Video Tape: **1**
● Section: **18.0**

DVD: **1**
Volume: **NA**
Menu Chapter: **18**
● Section: **18.0**

F.I.G.H.T. Tip:
Opposing Forces
Use opposing forces to increase the effect of your strikes. For example, when elbowing to the neck, push the head into the elbow with your opposite hand. When kneeing if possible push your opponent down into the knee. In many techniques, while one part of your body is striking, another will be in a position to create an opposing force.

Being in a self-defense or neutral stance essentially means standing normally as shown in **Picture 54**, or how you typically stand. You are more secure if your typical stance does not include having your hands in your pockets. Try to get in the habit of not keeping your hands in your pockets. You are not prepared to fight in this stance, however if you are attacked you will generally be in this very position. Your instinctive response to being attacked by surprise is a defensive response. In our system, this is immediately combined with an attack, converting defense into offense and into a fight. There are actually two other self-defense or neutral positions, sitting and lying down. In this series we will cover standing techniques only.

The most important element in the initial response to an attack is 'explosiveness'. If you are in a neutral stance, your attacker will have likely moved first to strike you. You must practice these few techniques

repeatedly to become fast enough that if you perceived the initial hostile motion of your attacker, you can actually depart second but arrive first. These are all clinch range techniques.

ELBOW TO THROAT
Target – Side of throat –Carotid Artery

1. Begin in neutral stance. **Picture 54**

2. Take a walking step with your left leg while simultaneously elbowing to the side of your attacker's neck with your right elbow. During practice, use your left hand as a target. In real self-defense situation your left hand would cup the opposite side of your attacker's throat and push it towards and into the elbow. **Picture 55**

3. Return to neutral stance when practicing. **Picture 54**

4. Practice this on both sides. It is essential to step in with the leg opposite the elbow being thrown. It is also essential to take a small natural step. A large step will lower your body and cause you to strike your attacker's chest. This is far less effective.

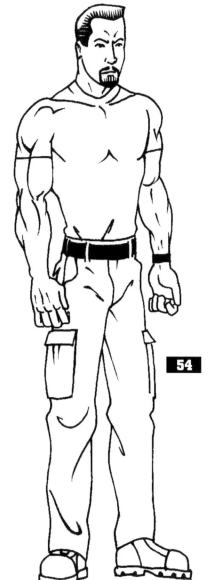

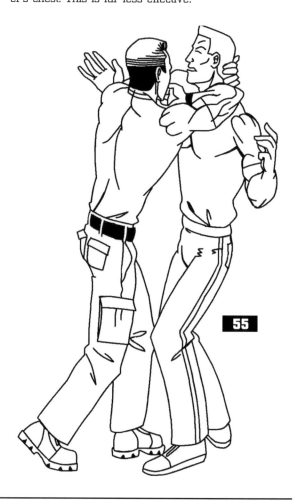

SIDE ELBOW

Primary Characteristic
Target – Head or Neck

1. Begin in neutral stance. **Picture 56**

2. Step sideways toward your attacker, moving <u>both</u> legs, while throwing an elbow straight to the side as shown in **Picture 58**. Ignore Picture 57.

3. Note that the opposite hand is placed by your neck. This protects your neck against an attack from a knife. We assume there is always a knife!

4. Do not move only the foot closest to your attacker, as this will lower your body and make your strike far less effective.

5. Return to neutral stance when practicing. **Picture 56**

ENTRAPPING ELBOW

Primary Characteristic
Target- Head or neck

1. Begin in neutral stance. **Picture 56**

2. Step one foot in front of the other and cover up as shown in **Picture 57** The step is a natural walking step. Again, do not take a large step as that will lower your body.

3. From the cover up, drop your rear hand to cover your neck and elbow straight to the side with your front hand as in **Picture 58**. Do not rotate. The elbow should not travel behind your back.

4. Return to neutral stance when practicing. **Picture 56**

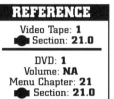

Fight Tip: Elbows
In the side elbow, you are simply stepping directly sideways and delivering the elbow to an attacker who is coming from the side. In the entrapping elbow your attacker is in front of you and you are stepping forward and turning sideways before elbowing.

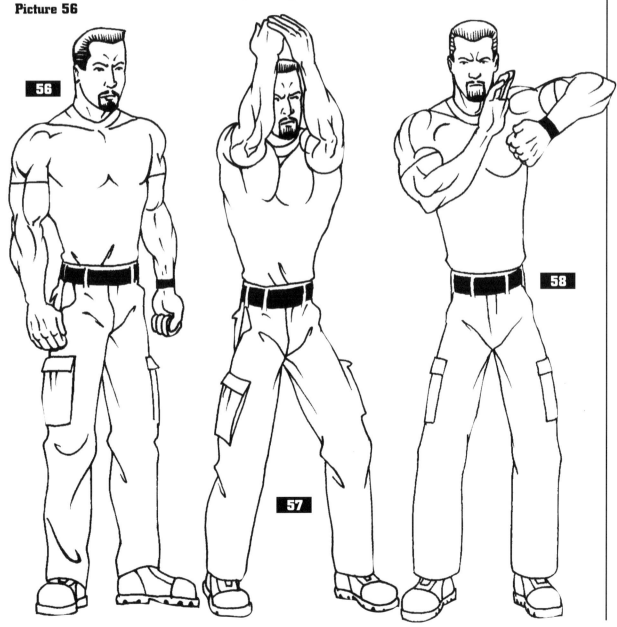

Self-Defense (Neutral) Stance Techniques

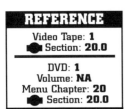

REFERENCE

Video Tape: **1**
◆ Section: **20.0**

DVD: **1**
Volume: **NA**
Menu Chapter: **20**
◆ Section: **20.0**

UPPERCUT ELBOW
Target- Under Chin

1. Begin in neutral stance. **Picture 59**

2. Rotate and pivot your right foot and simultaneously raise you elbow as if you are brushing your fingers through your hair on the right side as in **Picture 60**. While your elbow is coming up, your other hand protects your neck **Picture 61**.

3. This is designed to hit the attacker's chin when in close– the rotation is important to cause the elbow to be in the center of your (and, therefore, your attacker's) body. Do not take a step. If you picture your attacker right in front of you, if you take a step you will jam yourself into him rendering the technique ineffective.

4. Return to neutral stance when practicing. **Picture 59**

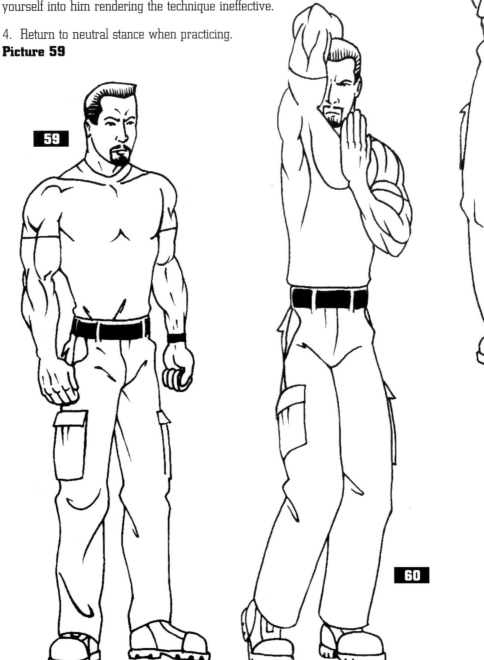

BACK ELBOW

Target- Ribcage

1. Begin in neutral stance. **Picture 62**

2. This is designed to be used when you are trapped in a bear-hug that overlaps your arms. Therefore, you have limited room to move. Keep this in mind when practicing and keep your motions tight and quick.

3. Rotate slightly and throw your elbow sharply back and slightly up. **Picture 63**. Be explosive. This is designed to loosen his hold on you.

4. Return to neutral stance when practicing. **Picture 62**

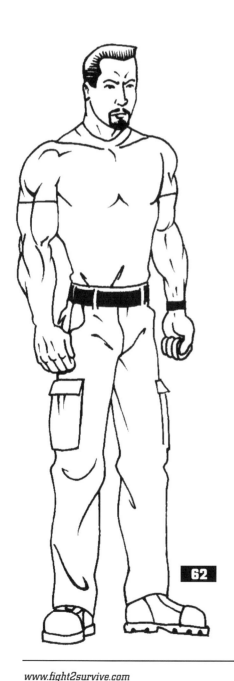

REFERENCE

Video Tape: **1**
Section: **22.0**

DVD: **1**
Volume: **NA**
Menu Chapter: **22**
Section: **22.0**

F.I.G.H.T. Tip:
Elbows
When delivering elbows, some people clench their hands into fists. Don't. Your elbow is a bone. Clenching your hands doesn't make it harder. It will, however, tense your muscles and detract from the elbow strike's power.

REFERENCE

Video Tape: **1**
◆ Section: **23.0**

DVD: **1**
Volume: **NA**
Menu Chapter: **23**
◆ Section: **23.0**

REFERENCE

Video Tape: **1**
◆ Section: **S3**

DVD: **1**
Volume: **NA**
Menu Chapter: **22-23**
◆ Section: **S3**

UPPERCUT ELBOW TO THE REAR

Target- Ribcage

1. Begin in neutral stance. **Picture 64**

2. This technique is designed to hit your attacker's chin hard when he is behind you.

3. Bump backwards with your rear while bending forward so that your attacker is pushed back and likely leans into you. **Picture 65**

4. Simultaneously rotate and bring your elbow up sharply behind you. The rotation must be enough so that your elbow is coming up the centerline of your (and hence your attacker's) body. Remember- your attacker was holding you from behind. Therefore his centerline and yours are the same. Your elbow will strike his chin from underneath. **Picture 65**

5. If you have ever played pool (billiards, snooker) this is very similar to the motion of your elbow prior to hitting the cue ball.

6. Return to neutral stance when practicing. **Picture 64**

SUMMARY

The strikes covered above should be practiced in front of a mirror, using both left and right-side leads, numerous times. If you can do this together with a training partner (not on each other, but side by side), you both will be able to carefully practice the self-defense scenarios that follow. Variations of these strikes and some simple additional elements will be introduced as needed.

F.I.G.H.T. Tip: Reaction Time

In this technique and some other techniques you need not look at your attacker if his position relative to you is known (ex., bear hug - rear uppercut elbow) and he has demonstrated his hostile intent. Looking will only create delayed reaction time and expose your intent.

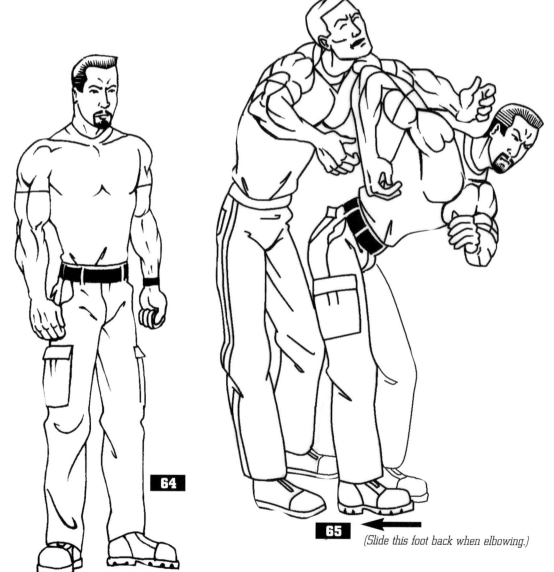

64

65 ⬅

(Slide this foot back when elbowing.)

Street Scenarios

It is impossible to anticipate every nuance of every way in which you might be attacked. Even if we could do so, it would take many years to train to respond uniquely to each one. We do not take that approach. The F.I.G.H.T. program's Haganah system is based on a common set of scenarios that represent the most likely types of attacks that you might encounter. If you learn these scenarios and practice them enough to program your responses into your neuromuscular system, your body will react to a given threat effectively and quickly. Each scenario is dealt with in a way that:

- assumes your instinctive response,
- builds on it leading to a counterattack, and
- brings you to a common point where your remaining counterattack is a choice of one of three, depending upon your ultimate objective.

The system does not fight your natural instincts, thereby allowing you to become programmed faster and to need less thought (which means quicker reaction times) to launch your counterattack. Also, by bringing all scenarios to a common point, the system enables you to require far less programming and enables you to build strong skills quickly in the crucial final phases of your techniques. It also enables you to have a goal if you are confronted by a scenario you have never experienced; that is to get to a common point (point of reference) and follow the steps associated with your ultimate objective to complete your counterattack. This will make more sense after you learn the attack scenarios. There are 18 hand-to-hand combat scenarios, nine gun threat scenarios, and nine knife attack scenarios. There are also three knife threat scenarios. The 18 hand-to-hand combat scenarios are:

1. Straight Punch-
2. Kick to Groin

Chokes (with variations)
3. Front- static
4. Front-pushing
5. Side-static
6. Side-pushing
7. Rear-pulling
8. Rear-pushing

Holds (with variations)
9. Rear bear-hug- arms pinned
10. Rear bear-hug- arms free
11. Lapel grab with punch
12. Lapel grab no punch

Headlocks
13. Side-high
14. Side-low
15. Rear-static
16. Rear-pulling

Tackles
17. Inside
18. Outside

As we review the 18 most common scenarios attackers use in a hand-to-hand situation, you will begin to see common patterns of defenses/counterattacks. Although initially there may seem to be a lot to learn, once you practice each several times and get through an entire rotation of them, you will see that the techniques you use build upon each other. Generally, each technique is executed in this sequence:

• **The Entry** - The entry is the first step and begins the sequence of overlapping moves. The entry is typically based on a natural instinctive reaction that is common, such as most people's tendency when a punch is thrown at them, to flinch and try to cover up or move. By using slight variations on instinctive reactions for the entry techniques, the system makes it easier for you to become programmed to react properly. You start out going with your instinct rather than fighting it.

• **The Counterattack** - This is the next few moves that are unique to the specific situation. The Haganah system uses as many common elements as possible during this phase of a technique to minimize programming time and your need to think about each step.

• **The Point of Reference and Objective** - This is the last part of each technique and there are only a few variations. By having common points of reference as described below and common counterattack strategies as you will see among many of these scenarios, you are able to achieve a programmed response state more quickly since each time you practice you may be practicing different scenarios but repeating common elements.

With practice, you will begin to develop instincts as to how to react and automatically follow through to a point of reference. Once you reach the point of reference, you are on familiar territory, regardless of the specific attack that was launched against you. This process can be greatly enhanced and accelerated by using the F.I.G.H.T. video series and even further enhanced (and added to with more advanced material) by attending F.I.G.H.T. intensive seminars. To purchase videos (if you have not already) and for more information on available seminars, go to *www.fight2survive.com.*

F.I.G.H.T. Tip: The Structure Of An Encounter
Most encounters begin as a self-defense reaction -- the entry. This is followed by a counterattack which requires fighting skills. F.I.G.H.T. will help you develop both. The entry and counter attack may be only a few moves in total. By becoming proficient at the Points of Reference and Objectives, you give yourself much more training time to develop strong initial self-defense reactions to a variety of scenarios and more time to develop improvisational skill in you initial self-defense reactions. Remember, the entire system works like a "funnel", normally bringing you to a familiar place (or a slight variation.)

REFERENCE
Video Tape: **1**
◀◼ Section: **34.0–39.0**

DVD: **1**
Volume: **NA**
Menu Chapter: **34–39**
◀◼ Section: **34.0–39.0**

At some point in each hand-to-hand combat scenario or engagement, your goal is to reach one of the three points of reference: right side control (POR #1), head control (POR #2), or left side control (POR #3). From each of these, you will be able to do what we call 'go to work', that is, execute a series of strikes and moves that either incapacitate or, if necessary, terminate your attacker. Let us examine each point of reference.

POR #1 AND POR #3
Right side control and Left side control

If executed on your right side it is POR #1, on your Left side it is POR #3

1. With your hand closest to your attacker (right if he is to your right), reach up over his shoulder, slap the center of his back hard to create damage and get a good grip, and grab the back of his shirt. Gather as much of his shirt in your hand as possible and yank it hard toward you. **Picture 66** (Right side shown).

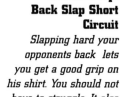

**F.I.G.H.T. Tip:
Back Slap Short
Circuit**
Slapping hard your opponents back lets you get a good grip on his shirt. You should not have to struggle. It also illustrates a F.I.G.H.T. Principle: Create pain to short circuit your opponent every time you touch him.

66

2. Put your forearm across the side of his face as shown in **Picture 67**, push out with your elbow and pull down. This will start to break his joint alignment and will keep him from effectively punching or kneeing you. If his arm is free, pin it to him with the hand position shown in the close-up **Picture 68**. This is the hand position you will use to pin his elbow to him. It keeps him from being able to move the arm enough to

67

deploy a weapon from that side. You might also end up at this point of reference with slightly different hand position (ex, he launched a punch, with his arm pinned to you instead of to him, as shown in **Picture 66**. All other elements are the same regardless of whether his arm is pinned to him

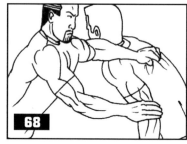

68

or pinned to you and exactly how it's held. It is just the pinning position that is different.

3. "Load up" to knee by bring your strong leg back. **Picture 66**

4. Knee three times. Load-up each time. Knee with opposite leg on the second and third knees. The target is anywhere low-line (lower abdomen or below). Ideally, the groin should be hit at least one time. **Picture 69, 70, and 71**

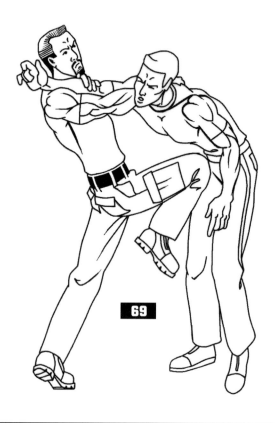

69

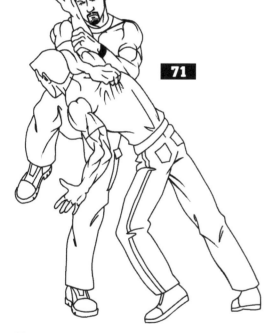

If his right leg is forward, this will be your right leg. If his left leg is forward, it will be your left leg. Place your thigh against his as shown in **Picture 72**. Using

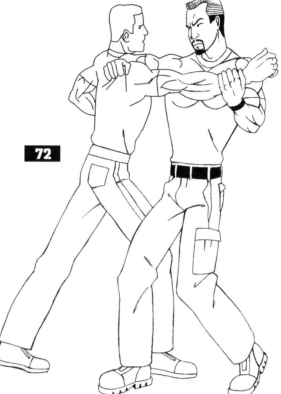

your forearm that is holding him to push forward and across, throw him down as shown in **Picture 73**.

F.I.G.H.T. Tip: Alternate Takedown

An alternative takedown is the 12/6 takedown. By lifting his arm which you have pinned to 12 o'clock and pistoning straight down with the wedge of your hand on the back of his neck to 6 o'clock, you will drop him right in front of you. This is simple and particularly effective in tight spaces. If he resists, hit first with your free hand or elbow.

F.I.G.H.T. TIP REFERENCE

Video Tape: **2**
◆ Section: **6.2**

DVD: **2**
Volume: **1**
Menu Chapter: **6**
◆ Section: **6.2**

5. You are now at a point where you can choose between three different options depending upon your objective: a takedown (restraining) option, an incapacitation option, or a termination option. **You** must make the appropriate choice based upon the specific situation and threat level.

6. If you choose to takedown and restrain your attacker, you will maintain contact with and control over the pinned arm through the takedown. Do not disconnect. Step through past his forward leg with your inside leg.

Points of Reference

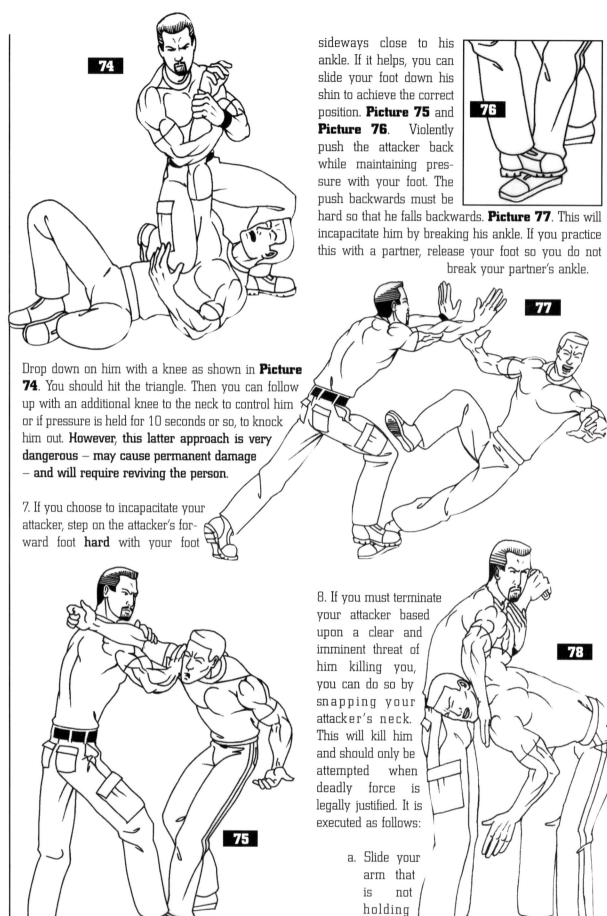

Drop down on him with a knee as shown in **Picture 74**. You should hit the triangle. Then you can follow up with an additional knee to the neck to control him or if pressure is held for 10 seconds or so, to knock him out. **However, this latter approach is very dangerous – may cause permanent damage – and will require reviving the person.**

7. If you choose to incapacitate your attacker, step on the attacker's forward foot **hard** with your foot sideways close to his ankle. If it helps, you can slide your foot down his shin to achieve the correct position. **Picture 75** and **Picture 76**. Violently push the attacker back while maintaining pressure with your foot. The push backwards must be hard so that he falls backwards. **Picture 77**. This will incapacitate him by breaking his ankle. If you practice this with a partner, release your foot so you do not break your partner's ankle.

8. If you must terminate your attacker based upon a clear and imminent threat of him killing you, you can do so by snapping your attacker's neck. This will kill him and should only be attempted when deadly force is legally justified. It is executed as follows:

    a. Slide your arm that is not holding his shirt down

IMPORTANT F.I.G.H.T. Warning:

Use of Force

If you incapacitate or terminate an attacker, you will be required to legally justify your use of force. Never continue attacking once your attacker ceases to be a threat. Never use excessive force.

the opposite side of his neck and under his chin. **Picture 78** Do not simply reach over to grab his chin as you may pass in front of his mouth and he may bite you.

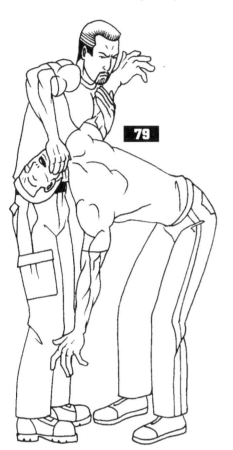

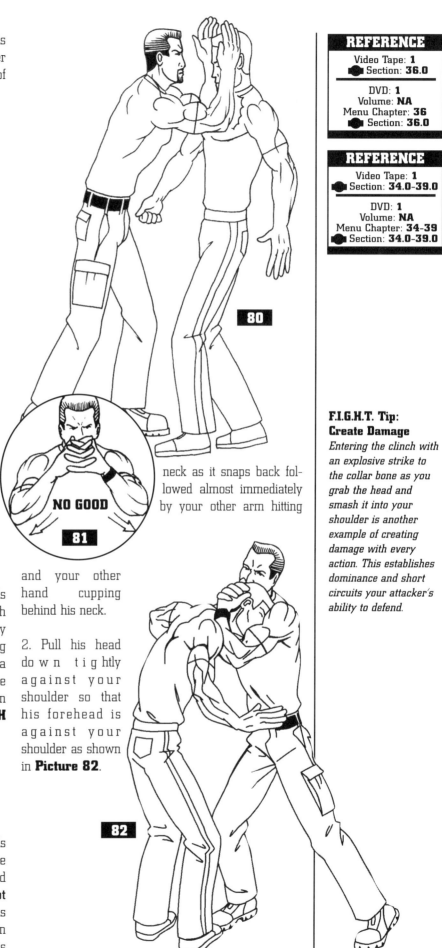

REFERENCE

Video Tape: **1**
◆ Section: **36.0**

DVD: **1**
Volume: **NA**
Menu Chapter: **36**
◆ Section: **36.0**

REFERENCE

Video Tape: **1**
◆ Section: **34.0-39.0**

DVD: **1**
Volume: **NA**
Menu Chapter: **34-39**
◆ Section: **34.0-39.0**

NO GOOD

b. Strongly wrench the head up and backwards as depicted in **Picture 79**. If you just wrench up, the head has a lot of side-to-side mobility and the neck may not snap, but by wrenching up and angling back, you are attacking in a direction with limited range of motion and are likely to snap the neck. This will result in death. **NEVER PRACTICE THIS WITH ANYONE.**

POR #2
Head Control (clinch)

1. With your attacker in front of you, shoot your hands up on either side of his head striking his collarbone with your forearms and wrapping your hands around the back of his neck as shown in **Picture 80**. Do not intertwine your fingers or keep your elbows apart as shown in picture **Picture 81**. Ideally, your strong arm will hit first with your strong hand cupping behind his

and your other hand cupping behind his neck.

2. Pull his head down tightly against your shoulder so that his forehead is against your shoulder as shown in **Picture 82**.

neck as it snaps back followed almost immediately by your other arm hitting

**F.I.G.H.T. Tip:
Create Damage**
Entering the clinch with an explosive strike to the collar bone as you grab the head and smash it into your shoulder is another example of creating damage with every action. This establishes dominance and short circuits your attacker's ability to defend.

Do this by bringing your elbows close together and 'pistoning down' with your arms as shown in **Picture 83**. Keep your elbows close so he cannot simply escape underneath **Picture 84**. Keep his forehead tight to your shoulder.

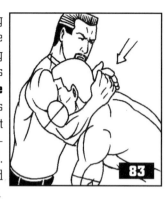

3. This is a 'Clinch'.

4. From this position, execute three knees as in step #4 in POR #1 or #3.

5. There are multiple options to achieve one of the three objectives from here:

a. To incapacitate you can break the ankle as in step # 7 in POR #1 or #3, or

b. You can rotate the person's head to turn him around facing away from you and then take-down (restrain), incapacitate, or terminate him.

F.I.G.H.T. Tip: "Loading Up"
Load up everytime you knee - bring the leg you intend to knee with back, then knee your opponent. This provides extra momentum and strength.

c. Rotation occurs by sliding one hand (preferably your dominant hand) down the neck and under the chin as shown in **Picture 85**, while moving the other hand a bit up the head to the opposite side of the crown of the head, and then, without letting the head disconnect from your body , spinning it as shown in **Picture 86**. The attacker will spin his body to follow his head. Your attacker is now positioned as shown in **Picture 87**. Keep him bent backward by keeping his head connected to your body throughout the turn.

d. After you have rotated your attacker,

you are behind him and have a strong psychological and leverage advantage. Your options are:

i. Drop him on your knee as in **Picture 88** causing a broken back, paralysis and possibly death

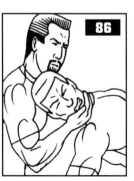

ii. Knee him in the spinal column achieving the same result

iii. Snap his neck by tilting it and wrenching your hands as shown in picture **Picture 89**

iv. Throw him to the ground by pushing behind his knee with your foot and pushing him forward violently as shown in **Picture 90**. This will slam his knee into the ground. You can incapacitate him by stepping on and breaking his ankle as shown in **Picture 91**.

All of the Points of reference and the alternative objectives are described in the videos and they include a drill to practice both the primary strikes and points of reference.

NEVER PRACTICE TERMINATION OR PARALYZING TECHNIQUES WITH ANYONE.

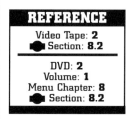

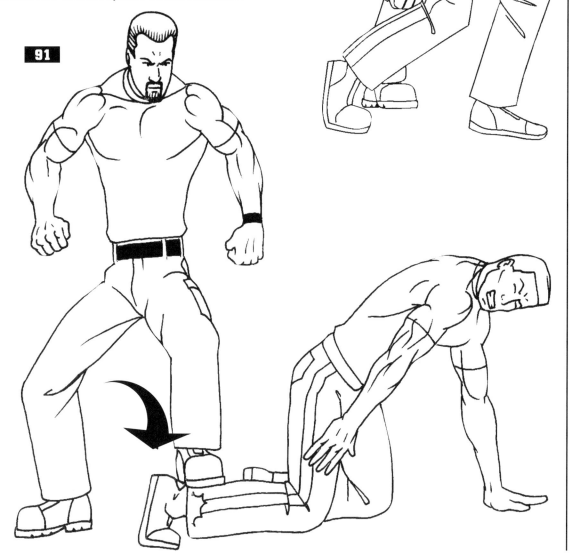

REFERENCE

Video Tape: **2**
◆ Section: **8.2**

DVD: **2**
Volume: **1**
Menu Chapter: **8**
◆ Section: **8.2**

This reference is for the takedown shown.

**IMPORTANT
F.I.G.H.T. WARNING:**

Head Turns

Rotating a person by turning their head is dangerous and can cause paralysis or death unintentionally. Use only if incapacitation or termination is legally justified. Practice gently and cautiously.

Street Scenarios

Street Attack 1 - Defense Against Straight Punch

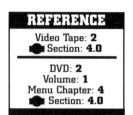

REFERENCE
Video Tape: **2**
◆ Section: **4.0**

DVD: **2**
Volume: **1**
Menu Chapter: **4**
◆ Section: **4.0**

Although some of these are practiced from a fighting stance, they can be executed from a neutral stance also.

PUNCHES AND KICKS

DEFENSE AGAINST STRAIGHT PUNCH
Primary Danger- Line of Fire (get out of the way)

1. Begin in fighting stance, left lead. **Picture 92**

2. As the punch is thrown, step to 11 o'clock. Move both feet. You have moved out of the line of fire. Your attacker's momentum is forward. His hand should pass you. **Picture 93**

3. While you are moving, check his arm with your forward hand. **Picture 93**. Be sure that you do not redirect him by bumping or pushing his arm away. The check is merely an added level of security against you getting hit. You want him to continue his motion straight forward. You are "dissolving" him into you.

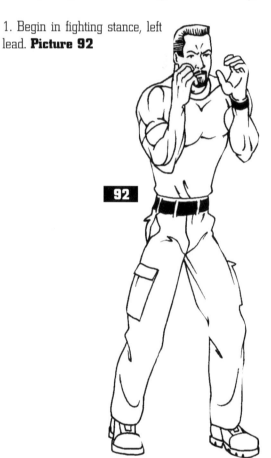

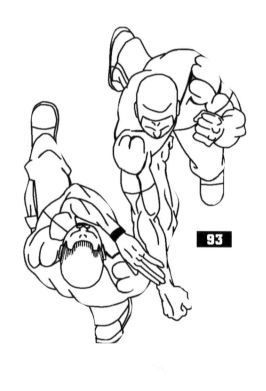

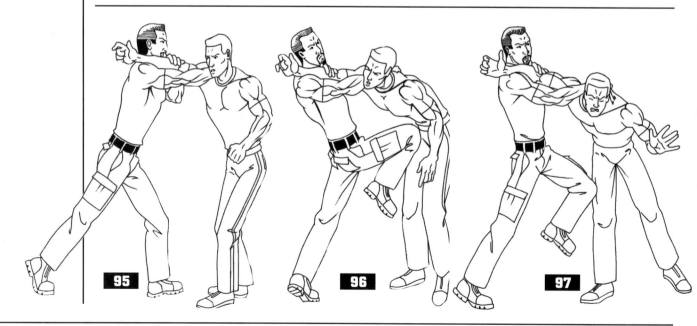

4. Strike his lower ribs with a rear hand punch. You do not need to aim. Since you moved to 11 o'clock, his ribs are accessible by you punching to your side at about a 90 degree angle. Practice not aiming, as your reaction time will be faster if you do not aim. **Picture 94**

5. With your rear hand, reach up slap his back hard and grab the back of his shirt. Gather as much shirt in your hand as possible. **Picture 95**

6. Put your arm across the side of his face and pull down somewhat. You have now reached point of reference #1 (POR # 1). You can go to work and choose your objective. Incapacitation is shown here. **Pictures 95-100.**

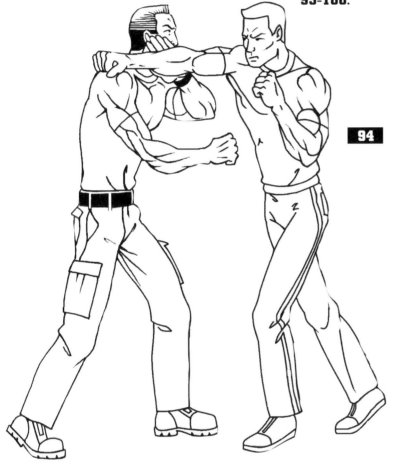

94

F.I.G.H.T. Tip: Pinning
If his arm doesn't end up easily pinned to you, pin it to him and continue. In this case, remember to pin it by his elbow to avoid him from freeing his arm.

98　　**99**　　**100**

Street Attack 2 - Defense Against Kick To The Groin

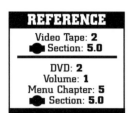

REFERENCE
Video Tape: **2**
◆ Section: **5.0**

DVD: **2**
Volume: **1**
Menu Chapter: **5**
◆ Section: **5.0**

DEFENSE AGAINST KICK TO THE GROIN

Primary Danger- Line of Fire (get out of the way)

1. Begin in fighting stance, left lead. **Picture 101**

2. When your attacker kicks, step to 11 o'clock. Move both feet ensuring that your rear leg swings back a little also to clear the kick. You are now out of the line of fire. Your attacker's momentum is forward. His foot should pass you. **Picture 102**

3. As you step off to 11 o'clock, check his leg with your forward hand. **Picture 103**. Be sure that you do not re-direct him by bumping or pushing his arm away. The check is merely an added level of security against you getting hit. You want him to continue his motion straight forward. You are dissolving him into you.

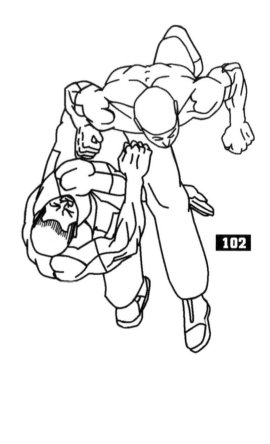

102

101

F.I.G.H.T. Note:
This Point of Reference is shown from the opposite side for illustration purposes. The opponent would actually be to your right.

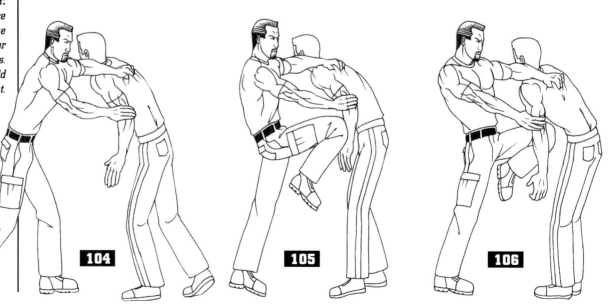

104   105   106

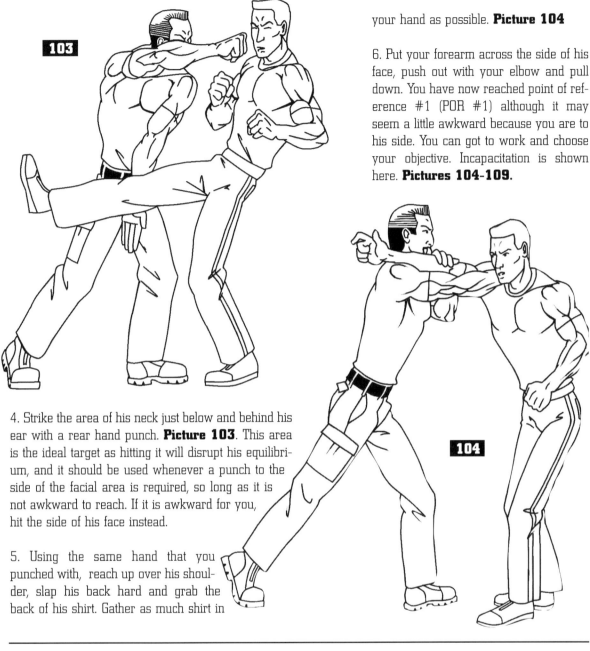

103

104

your hand as possible. **Picture 104**

6. Put your forearm across the side of his face, push out with your elbow and pull down. You have now reached point of reference #1 (POR #1) although it may seem a little awkward because you are to his side. You can got to work and choose your objective. Incapacitation is shown here. **Pictures 104-109**.

F.I.G.H.T. Tip: Pinning Arm

In the point of reference, his arm may end up pinned to your body or if it swings free you may have to pin it to his body as shown on page 46, picture 68. Even its specific position when pinned to you may vary. It doesn't matter as long as it is secure. Also, if you have it pinned to you before you get to the point of reference, keep it there. Don't disconnect.

4. Strike the area of his neck just below and behind his ear with a rear hand punch. **Picture 103**. This area is the ideal target as hitting it will disrupt his equilibrium, and it should be used whenever a punch to the side of the facial area is required, so long as it is not awkward to reach. If it is awkward for you, hit the side of his face instead.

5. Using the same hand that you punched with, reach up over his shoulder, slap his back hard and grab the back of his shirt. Gather as much shirt in

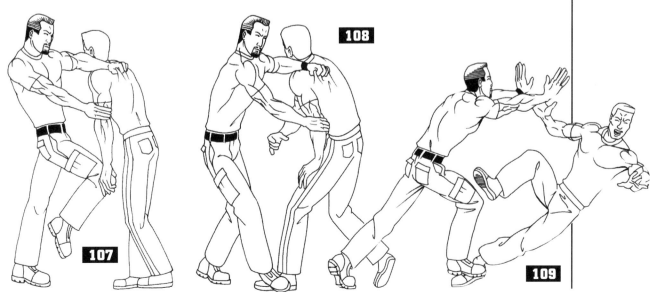

107

108

109

Front Choke - Static

REFERENCE
Video Tape: **2**
◆ Section: **6.0**
DVD. **2**
Volume: **1**
Menu Chapter: **6**
◆ Section: **6.0**

CHOKES

A choke occurs when your attacker places his hands around your throat. The choke can be from the front, side or rear. It can be static (no pushing or pulling) or can involve pushing or pulling. Each case is slightly different as you will see.

FRONT CHOKE- STATIC
Primary Danger- Thumbs on your Throat (remove the thumbs)

1. You are being choked as shown in **Picture 110**.

F.I.G.H.T. Tip: Unplugging
When unplugging, make sure you cup your hands and use them like hooks. Your thumbs should be pressed against the side of your hands. Do not try to wrap your thumbs around the opponent's wrists.

2. You will simultaneously 'unplug' the attacker's hands from your throat and lean back while shooting a knee to the groin as in **Picture 111**. Do **not** release your attacker's hands. Remember- you want your attacker close so you can go to work and if you have his hands 'welded' to your body, they can't hurt you or deploy a weapon.

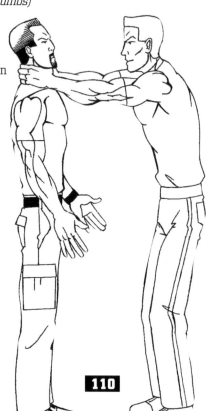

110

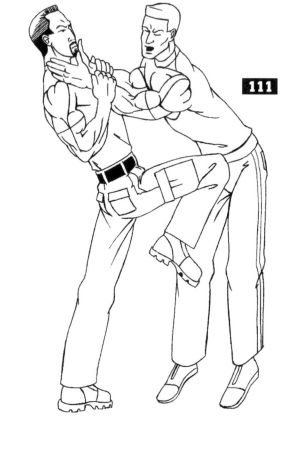

111

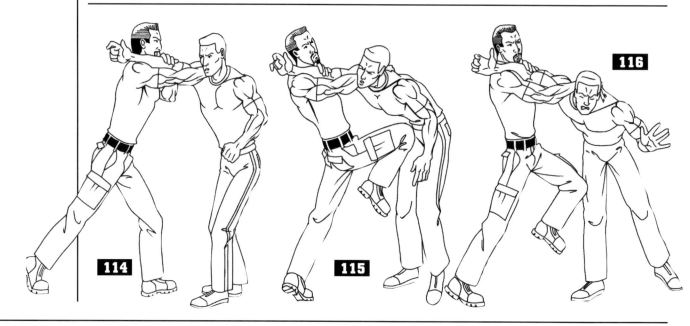

114

115

116

3. The unplugging element consists of using your hands as hooks to sharply and tightly pulling **down and out** on your attacker's wrists as shown in **Picture 112**. It is important to practice unplugging not only for this scenario but also because it is used in other scenarios.

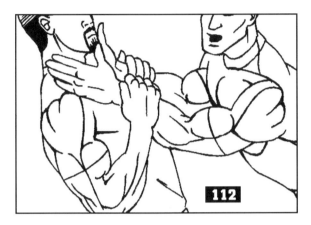

4. After the knee, elbow with your strong side arm while maintaining your pin on the other arm as shown in **Picture 113**.

5. You are positioned to go on to point of reference 1, or 3 and choose your objective. Continuing to POR #1 with incapacitation is shown here. **Pictures 114-119**.

F.I.G.H.T. Tip:
You can maintain his hand pinned to you as illustrated in the point of reference or you can pin it to him.

REFERENCE

Video Tape: **2**
⬡ Section: **7.0**

DVD. **2**
Volume: **1**
Menu Chapter: **7**
⬡ Section: **7.0**

FRONT CHOKE- PUSHING

Primary Danger- Loss of balance (Re-base yourself)

1. You are being choked as shown in **Picture 120**. Your attacker is pushing you backwards. Even though his thumbs are on your throat and he may be squeezing hard enough to cut of your air supply, the choke is not the primary danger. You are off balance. You cannot do anything effective when off balance. Worse yet, you may be thrown or fall to the ground. If so, the situation becomes far more complex. Therefore the primary danger is losing your balance and going to the ground. Despite the discomfort caused by the attacker's choke hold, don't panic. You have time to break his hold, but first you must regain your balance.

2. Turn sideways with your weak-side foot back and plant it firmly as shown in **Picture 120**. This stabilizes you quickly.

**F.I.G.H.T. Tip:
Pinning Arm**

In the point of reference, his arm may end up pinned to your body or if it swings free you may have to pin it to his body as shown on page 46, picture 68. Even its specific position when pinned to you may vary. It doesn't matter as long as it is secure. Also, if you have it pinned to you before you get to the point of reference, keep it there. Don't disconnect.

The parties in this point of reference have been rotated for illustration purposes.

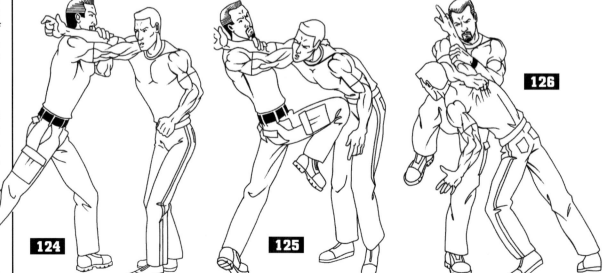

3. Raise your strong-side arm (right-handed shown) straight up keeping it close to your ear as shown **Picture 121**. Then, piston your arm straight down while simultaneously using your other hand to hug your chest. See **Picture 122**. This movement is similar to the Entrapping Elbow that you practiced in the Fundamental Strikes section. It will do several things; it will break your attackers hold, it will position you for an elbow to the attacker's face and it may enable you to 'trap' your attacker's hands against your chest. You

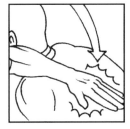

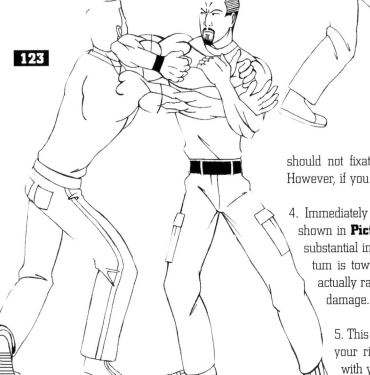

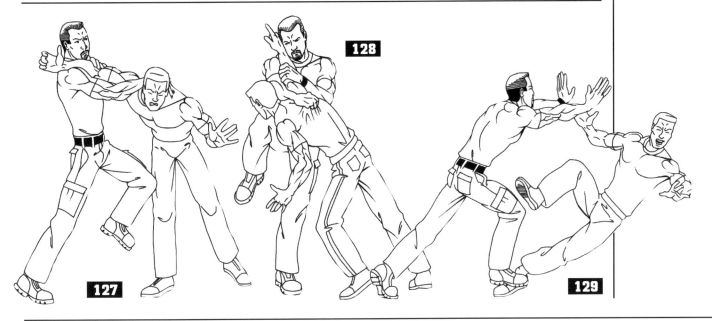

**F.I.G.H.T. Tip:
POR Reminder**
When entering the point of reference:

• *Reach over the shoulder and slap the center of his back hard*

• *Gather as much shirt (or skin) as possible*

• *Yank toward you*

• *Put your forearm across the side of his face*

• *Apply downward pressure*

should not fixate on trapping your attacker's hands. However, if you trap them, consider it a bonus.

4. Immediately elbow strike your attacker's face as shown in **Picture 123**. The elbow strike will have substantial impact because your attacker's momentum is toward you (he was pushing) so he will actually ram his face into the elbow, doubling the damage.

5. This will enter POR #1 if you elbowed with your right hand or POR #3 if you elbowed with your left hand. POR #1 is shown. Go to work. **Pictures 124-129.**

REFERENCE
Video Tape: **2**
◆ Section: **8.0**

DVD: **2**
Volume: **1**
Menu Chapter: **8**
◆ Section: **8.0**

SIDE CHOKE- STATIC

Primary Danger - Thumbs on Throat (remove them)

1. You are being choked as shown in **Picture 130**.

2. You will drop down by quickly opening your legs and simultaneously unplug the attacker's front hand (left if he is to your right or vice versa) as shown in **Picture 131**.

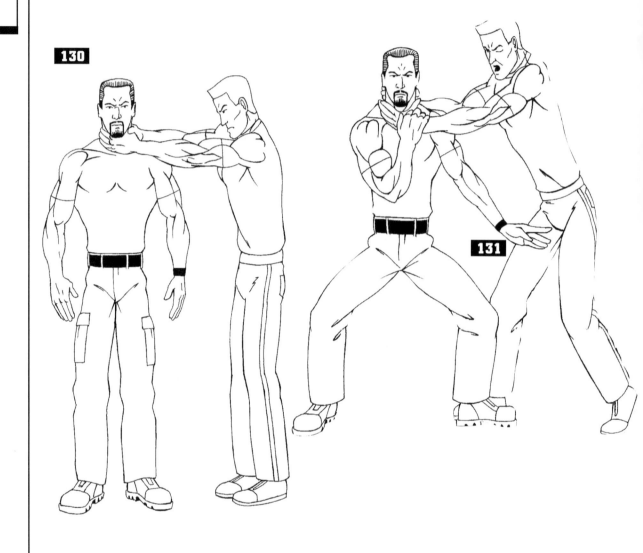

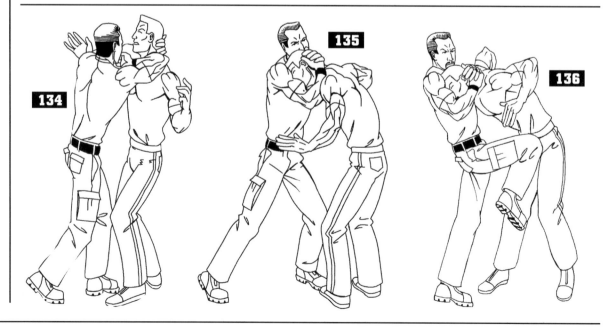

3. Immediately after unplugging the attacker's hand, execute a groin slap with your free hand as shown in **Picture 131**.

4. Rise up by bringing your outside leg towards your inside leg and execute an uppercut elbow to the side, striking under the chin as shown in **Picture 132**.

5. Step off to the side and turn in, as shown in **Picture 133**, while wrapping your inside arm around the back of his neck and delivering an elbow strike with your opposite arm to the side of your attacker's neck or head. You can now enter either outside point of reference (1 or 3 depending upon which elbow you struck with), or the inside point of reference #2 (clinch). This clinch is ideal.

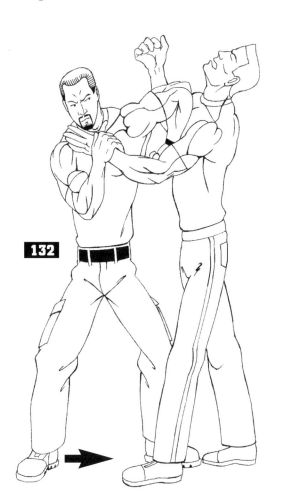

6. From there, reach around his neck with the arm you just used to elbow and clinch. You have entered POR 2. Choose your objective and go to work. **Pictures 134-139**

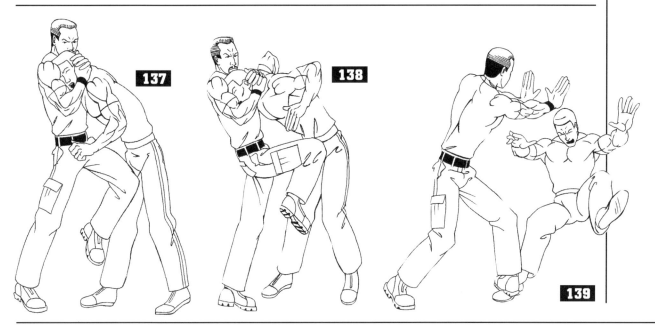

Side Choke - Pushing

REFERENCE

Video Tape: **2**
◆ Section: **9.0**

DVD: **2**
Volume: **1**
Menu Chapter: **9**
◆ Section: **9.0**

SIDE CHOKE- PUSHING
Primary Danger- Loss of balance (Re-base yourself)

1. You are being choked as shown in **Picture 140**. Your attacker is pushing you sideways. Once again, even though his thumbs are on your throat and he may be squeezing hard enough to cut of your air supply, that is not the primary danger. You are off balance. Remember, you can't do anything effective when off balance. Worse yet, you may be thrown or fall to the ground. If so, the situation becomes far more complex. That is the primary danger. Despite the discomfort, don't panic. You have time to break his hold. First you must regain your balance.

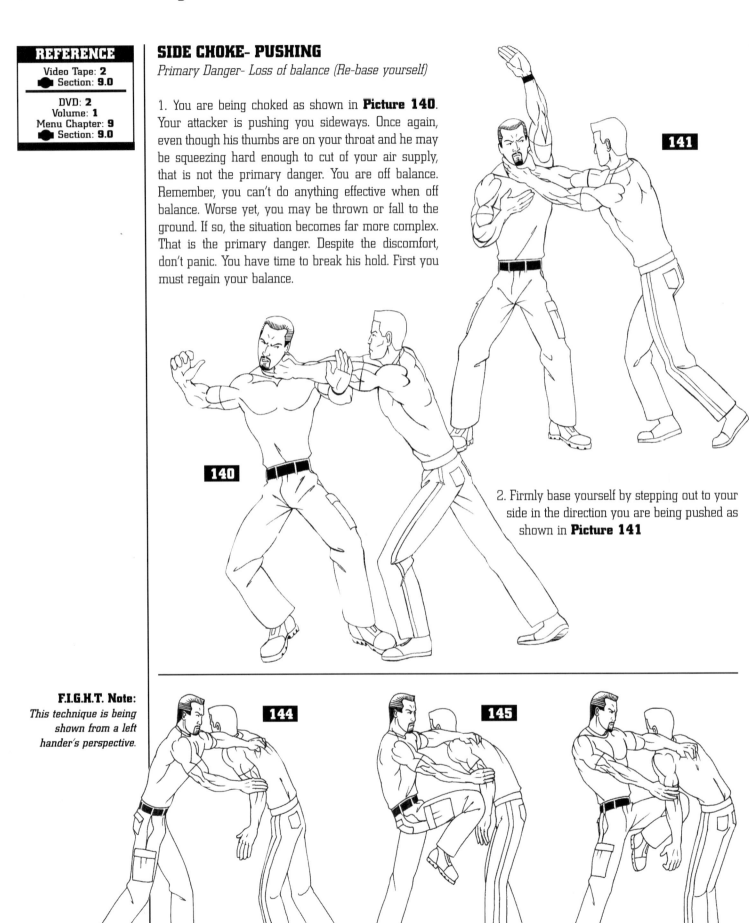

2. Firmly base yourself by stepping out to your side in the direction you are being pushed as shown in **Picture 141**

F.I.G.H.T. Note:
This technique is being shown from a left hander's perspective.

3. Raise your arm that is closest to your attacker, making sure you bring your arm to the outside of your attacker's arms and that your shoulder is close to your ear; twist slightly to the inside and piston your arm **straight down** while almost simultaneously hugging your chest with your other arm (this should occur slightly later) as shown in **Pictures 141 and 142**. This will remove his choke using a different unplugging tactic and likely trap his hands. It is important that your trap with the other hand be slightly delayed, otherwise you are actually holding his front arms in place while you try to unplug. You will be fighting against yourself.

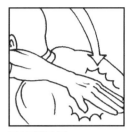

143

142

4. This movement is similar to the Entrapping Elbow that you practiced in the Fundamental Strikes section and nearly the same as the one that you used against the front choke – pushing.

5. Immediately, throw your elbow into your attacker's face as shown in **Picture 143**. This should have substantial impact because your attacker's momentum is toward you (he was pushing) so he will actually ram his face into the elbow, doubling the damage.

6. If you did trap his hand(s), use POR #1 if you elbowed with your right hand and POR #3 if you elbowed with your left hand. If not, you can use either the appropriate side POR or the clinch (POR #2). POR #1 is shown. Choose your objective and go to work. Incapacitation is shown. **Pictures 144-149**

**F.I.G.H.T. Tip:
POR Reminder**
When entering the point of reference:

• *Reach over the shoulder and slap the center of his back hard*

• *Gather as much shirt (or skin) as possible*

• *Yank toward you*

• *Put your forearm across the side of his face*

• *Apply downward pressure*

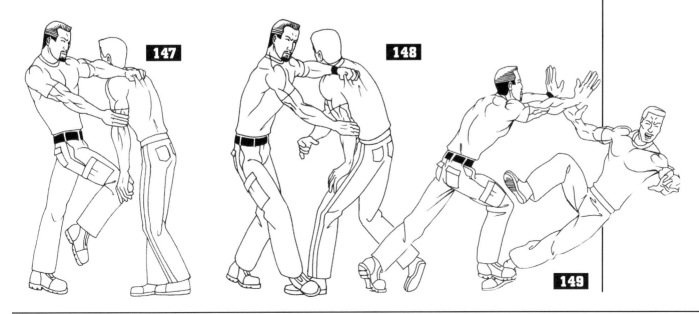

147   148   149

REFERENCE

Video Tape: **2**
◆ Section: **11.0**

DVD. **2**
Volume: **1**
Menu Chapter: **11**
◆ Section: **11.0**

REAR CHOKE- PULLING
Primary Danger- Loss of Balance (rebase yourself)

1. You are being choked as shown in **Picture 150**. Your attacker is pulling you backwards. Once again, even though his thumbs are on your throat and may be squeezing hard enough to cut of your air supply, that is not the primary danger. You are off balance. Remember, you can't do anything effective when off balance. Worse yet, you may be thrown or fall to the ground. If so, the situation becomes far more complex. That is the primary danger. Despite the discomfort, don't panic. You have time to break his hold. First you must regain your balance.

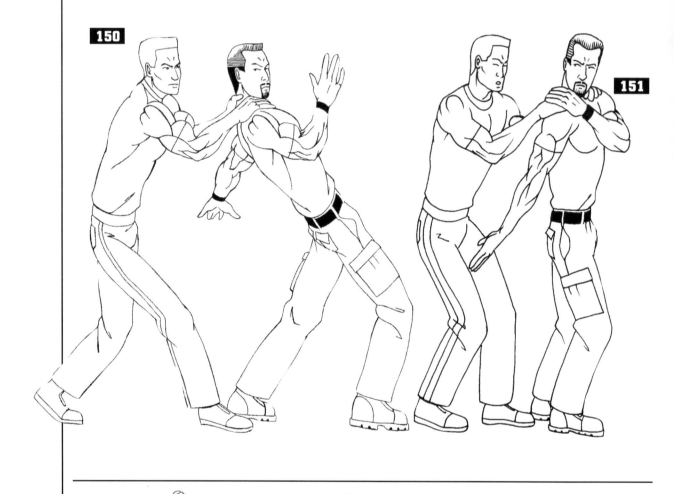

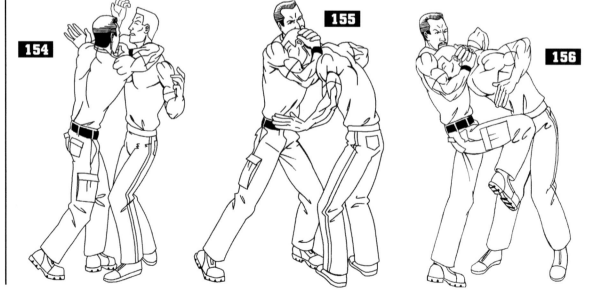

F.I.G.H.T. Note:
Images are rotated for illustration purposes.

2. With your left foot, step backwards to 7 o'clock as shown in **Picture 151**. Also as shown, simultaneously plug his right hand to you using your left hand. Remember, you are hooking his hand, not grabbing it.

3. With your right hand deliver a groin slap as also shown in **Picture 151**.

4. Deliver an uppercut elbow to the rear (same as you did in the fundamental strikes) shown in **Picture 152**

5. Turn into him as shown in **Picture 153**. Note the foot position..

6. You are now at POR #2. Go to work. **Pictures 154-159**

**F.I.G.H.T. Tip:
Cover Up**
Whenever you turn into an attacker who is behind you, cover up (hand on forehand).

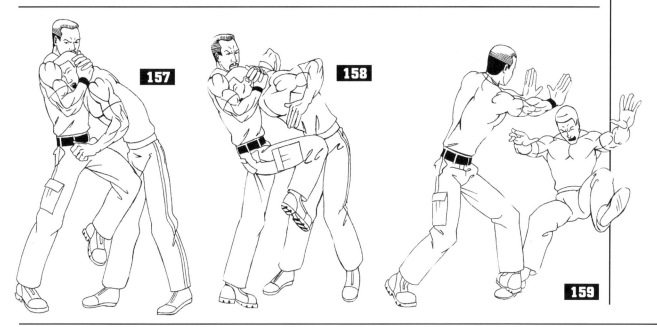

REFERENCE
Video Tape: **2**
◆ Section: **10.0**
DVD. **2**
Volume: **1**
Menu Chapter: **10**
◆ Section: **10.0**

REAR CHOKE – PUSHING

Primary Danger – Loss of Balance/Slamming into Something (rebase yourself)

1. You are being choked as shown in **Picture 160**. Your attacker is pushing you forwards. This might be to push you down or to push you into something such as a wall. You must get control of your balance.

2. Step firmly forward with your strong side foot like you are stepping on a bug. **Picture 160**. This will stabilize your balance. Raise your strong side arm straight up bringing your shoulder close to your ear as shown in **Picture 161**.

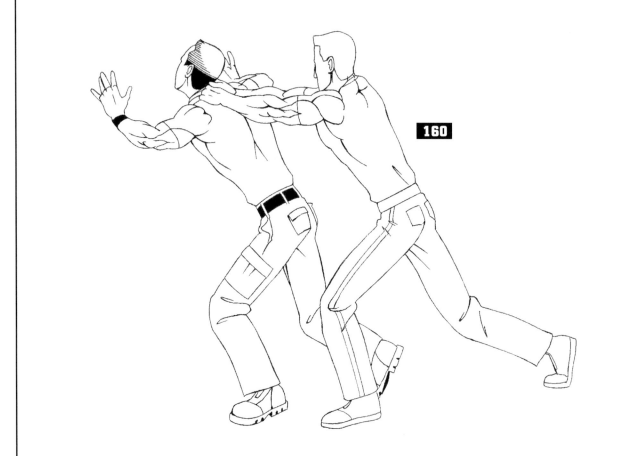

F.I.G.H.T. Note:
This technique is being shown from a left hander's perspective.

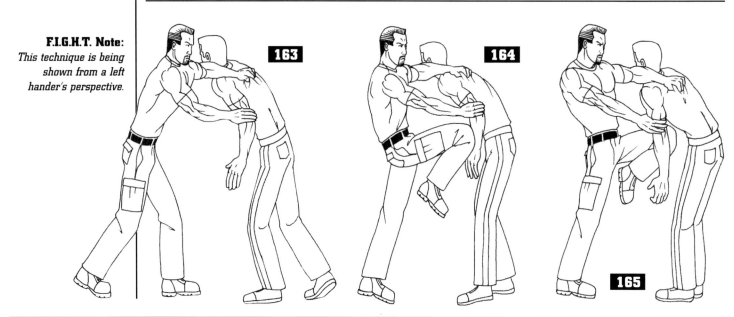

3. Exchange the position of your feet and turn in place as indicated in **Picture 161**. Your rear foot moves first. This will unplug his hands. Using your left hand, hit with a hammer fist* to the neck area (triangle) beneath and behind your attacker's ear as shown, or wherever your arm falls.

4. From there, reach over and slap his back gathering up his shirt and enter POR 1 (or POR 3 if he is to your left and you did this left handed). Go to work. **Pictures 163-168**

Holds - Rear Bear Hug - Arms Pinned

REFERENCE

Video Tape: **2**
◆ Section: **12.0**

DVD: **2**
Volume: **1**
Menu Chapter: **12**
◆ Section: **12.0**

REAR BEAR HUG – ARMS PINNED

Primary danger- Being thrown to the floor

1. You are being held from behind as shown in **Picture 169**. Note that your arms are pinned. You must escape quickly.

2. Turn slightly and slap at the groin from underneath as shown in **Picture 170**. Remember, the groin slap is with a loose wrist and open hand. You can slap from either side and do it a couple of times if you are not sure you made proper contact. This will loosen him up a bit.

F.I.G.H.T. Tip: Entry Strikes
It is best to execute the 3 self-defense entry strikes with your strong side arm.

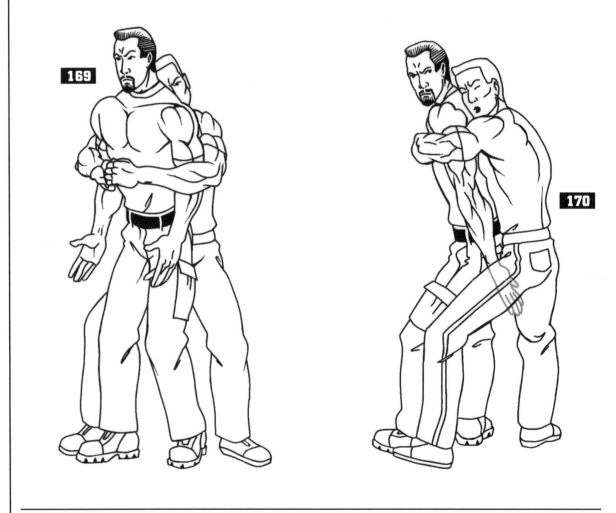

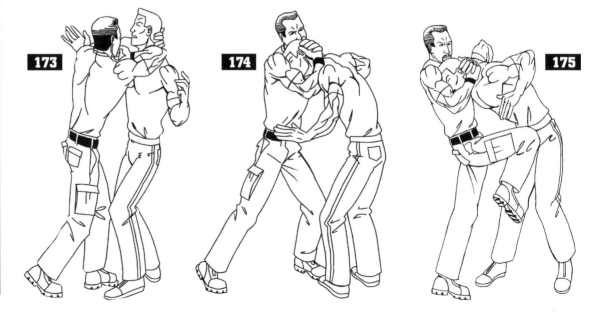

3. Deliver a rear elbow as shown in **Picture 171**. Remember to rotate slightly so that you hit him. If you do not rotate, you will elbow straight back by your side and miss your attacker. This strike will loosen him up a bit more.

5. Turn around in the direction of the side that you elbowed from and deliver an elbow to the neck a shown in **Picture 173**. Enter POR #2 (clinch). Choose your objective and go to work. Incapacitation shown. **Pictures 173-174.**

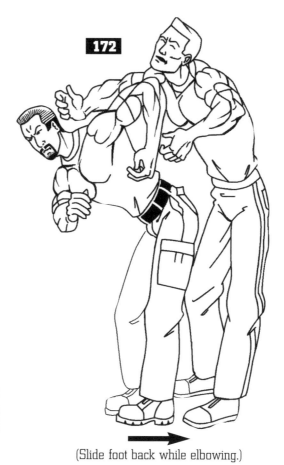

4. From the same side, deliver an uppercut elbow to the rear as practiced in fundamental strikes and shown in **Picture 172**. This will keep him off balance and allow you to enter a point of reference.

(Slide foot back while elbowing.)

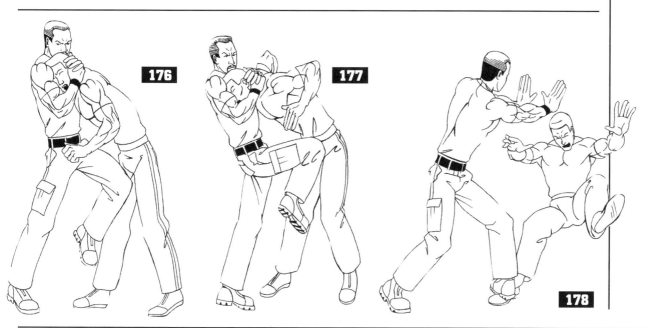

Holds - Rear Bear Hug - Arms Not Pinned

REFERENCE
Video Tape: **3**
◆ Section: **1.0**

DVD: **2**
Volume: **2**
Menu Chapter: **1**
◆ Section: **1.0**

REAR BEAR HUG – ARMS NOT PINNED

Primary danger- Being thrown to the floor

1. You are being held from behind as shown in **Picture 179**. Note that your arms are free. You must escape quickly.

F.I.G.H.T. Tip: Sliding Down The Arm

You are sliding your hands down his arms to grab the top hand rather than trying to identify which hand is on top as a way to ensure that the technique works in all environments (ex., low light). Then you can "peel" off his hand.

2. Deliver a rapid hard knock-knock strike to the back of your attacker's hands to loosen them up as shown in **Picture 180** and **Picture 181** If they don't loosen, do it again, but don't do it so many times that he completely disconnects.

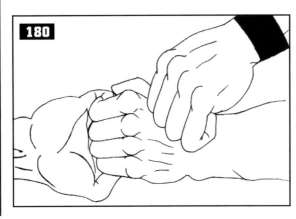

3. Put your hands on his forearms and slide down to his fingers as shown in **Picture 181**. His top hand will determine which of your hands slide under his fingers and which ends up at his wrist.

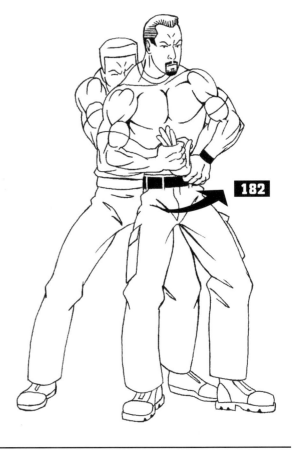

Gather up his fingers like you are 'peeling' them off your arm as shown in **Picture 182** and squeeze them tightly as shown. Keep your opposite hand on the back of his wrist as shown.

4. Execute a tight turn into him in the direction of your hand that is on the back of his wrist as shown in **Picture 182** and simultaneously bend his hand backwards as shown in **Picture 183**. Point his fingers directly at the centerline of his body. Push down hard. His joint alignment will break and he will buckle to his knees.

5. Knee him in the face as shown in **Picture 184**. Then deliver two additional knees anywhere. You can finish this off by applying so much pressure after he has buckled that you break his fingers and/or wrist and if his ankle is positioned as shown in **Picture 185** by breaking his ankle. Then push him to the ground and escape, or you can choose to restrain or terminate him (not explained).

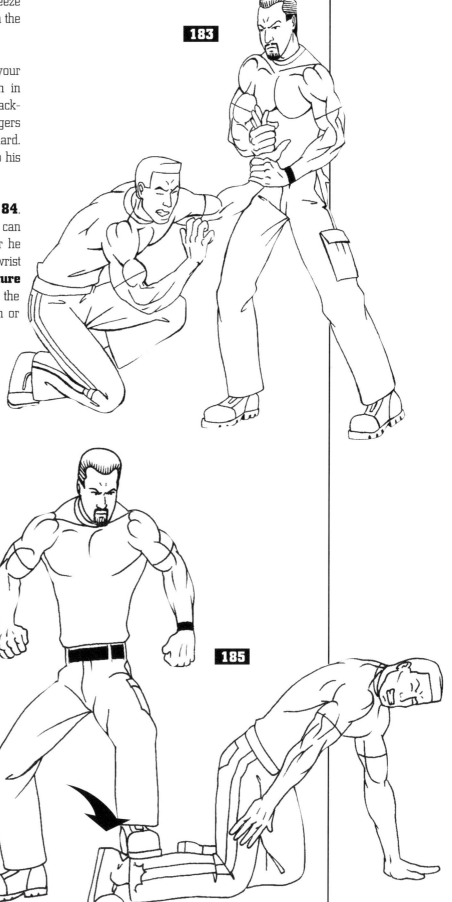

Lapel Grab - Before Punch

REFERENCE

Video Tape: **3**
◆ Section: **2.0**

DVD: **2**
Volume: **2**
Menu Chapter: **2**
◆ Section: **2.0**

**F.I.G.H.T. Tip:
Groin Kick**

*When you execute the
groin kick, his height
will determine where
your leg connects –
knee, shin, foot.*

LAPEL GRAB- BEFORE PUNCH

Primary Danger- The other hand striking

1. Your attacker grabs your shirt as shown in **Picture 186**. As we have said, this normally occurs

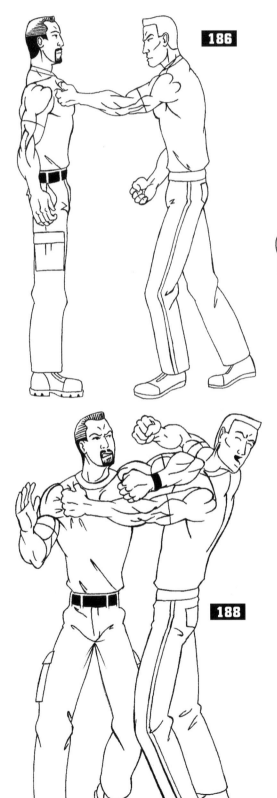

as a prelude to him throwing a punch or worse yet, beginning a stab with a knife. In this case we are assuming that his free arm is not yet in motion, so you have a chance to react to the grab itself.

2. Pick up your leg opposite the side he grabs you and strike under his groin hitting it with your shin (or near your foot if he has a long reach) as shown in **Picture 187**. Do not aim for the groin- there is no need to as he is right in front of you. Simply swing your leg quickly up and into it. Do not retract on contact; after kicking the groin simply let your foot fall into a forward step.

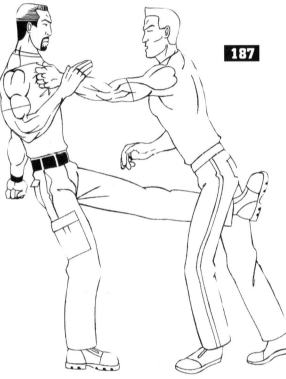

3. As you finish the kick, elbow him with your kicking side arm as shown in **Picture 188**. Upon completing the elbow, pin plugging his hand to your shirt with your hand as shown in **Picture 189A**.

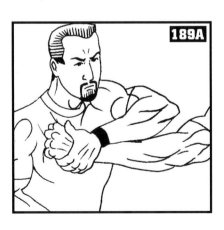

4. Swing your leg that is on the same side as your plugging hand back turning yourself sideways as shown in **Picture 189** and slightly rotate his hand downward while keeping it plugged to your shirt as shown in **Pictures 189A and B** (in F.I.G.H.T. Tip).

5. Piston down on the back of his upper arm just above the elbow as shown in **Picture 189**. This will break his joint alignment and cause him to buckle to the ground.

6. Knee him in the face and body, two or three times as shown in **Picture 190 and 191**.

7. Choose your objective. A variation of the ankle break is shown in **Picture 192**.

**F.I.G.H.T. Tip:
Proper Rotation**
You have properly rotated your attacker's arm if his elbow is pointing straight up. Do not over-rotate his arm. Also, keep his hand pinned to you as you rotate it as shown.

Piston straight down on his arm above to break his joint alignment and cause him to buckle to the ground. You can also restrain or terminate from this position.

REFERENCE

Video Tape: **3**
◆ Section: **3.0**

DVD: **2**
Volume: **2**
Menu Chapter: **3**
◆ Section: **3.0**

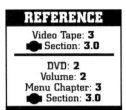

LAPEL GRAB – WITH A PUNCH

Primary Danger – The Punch

1. The attacker grabs your shirt as shown in **Picture 193**. This normally occurs as a prelude to him throwing a punch or worse yet, beginning a stab with a knife. In this case we are assuming that a punch has been thrown before you had a chance to react to the grab itself.

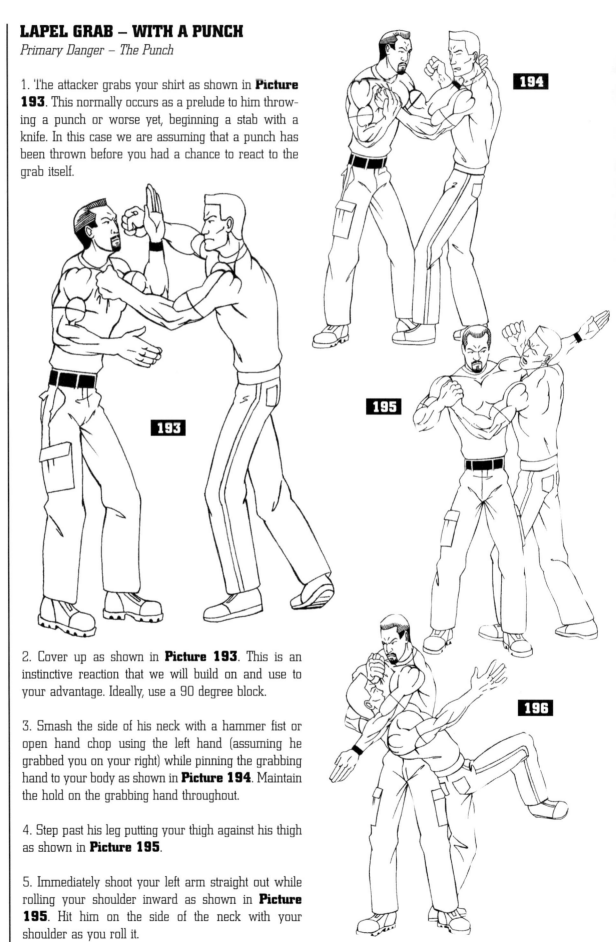

F.I.G.H.T. Tip:
Tight position on your thigh in Step #4 is important. Equally important is hitting him with your arm in the process of spiraling down in Step #5. The hit short circuits your opponent and makes the takedown easier.

2. Cover up as shown in **Picture 193**. This is an instinctive reaction that we will build on and use to your advantage. Ideally, use a 90 degree block.

3. Smash the side of his neck with a hammer fist or open hand chop using the left hand (assuming he grabbed you on your right) while pinning the grabbing hand to your body as shown in **Picture 194**. Maintain the hold on the grabbing hand throughout.

4. Step past his leg putting your thigh against his thigh as shown in **Picture 195**.

5. Immediately shoot your left arm straight out while rolling your shoulder inward as shown in **Picture 195**. Hit him on the side of the neck with your shoulder as you roll it.

6. Immediately (the second you hit him) windmill down, drawing a circle with your arm and throwing him to the ground. Keep the trapped hand pinned to your body during the throw as shown in **Picture 196**. This is called a spiral takedown.

7. You can either:
   a. 'Stretch him out' as shown in **Pictures 197, 198, 199, and 200** and kick him in the back (kidney) or head as necessary or

b. Drop a knee on his ribs and hit area below his ear (or head if necessary) as shown in **Picture 201 and 202** and if necessary stretch him out and follow up with kicks or hit him until you are confident that he is no longer a threat.

8. Stretching him out means pulling his arm hard enough to drag him. You should be above his shoulder-line .

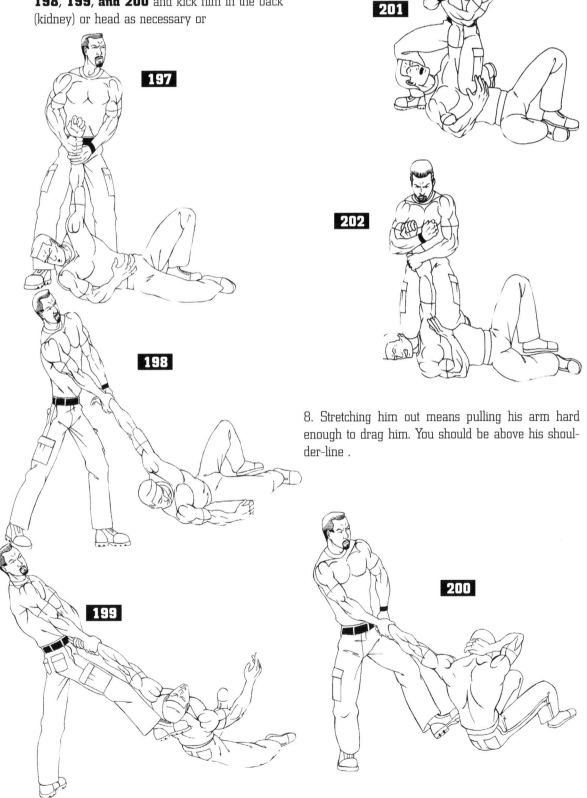

Headlocks - Side Headlock - High Position

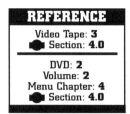

REFERENCE
Video Tape: **3**
Section: **4.0**

DVD: **2**
Volume: **2**
Menu Chapter: **4**
Section: **4.0**

A headlock occurs when the attacker wraps his arm around your neck as shown in **Picture 203**. He can be positioned in a number of ways (to your side, rear, leaning etc), and he can use his opposite arm in a number of different ways (holding his wrist or hand, holding your head, free).

SIDE HEADLOCK – HIGH POSITION
Primary Danger – His Free Hand

1. You are being held as shown in **Picture 203**. Even though there may be pressure on your throat and he may be squeezing hard enough to restrict your air supply or blood flow, his free hand is the primary danger. By punching you repeatedly in the face, his free hand can cause enough damage to render you ineffective. Despite the headlock's discomfort, don't panic. You have time to break his hold, but you must act quickly to neutralize his free hand.

2. Put your opposite side hand between his hand and your face as shown in **Picture 203** At the same time, with your other hand, reach around his back and secure his elbow

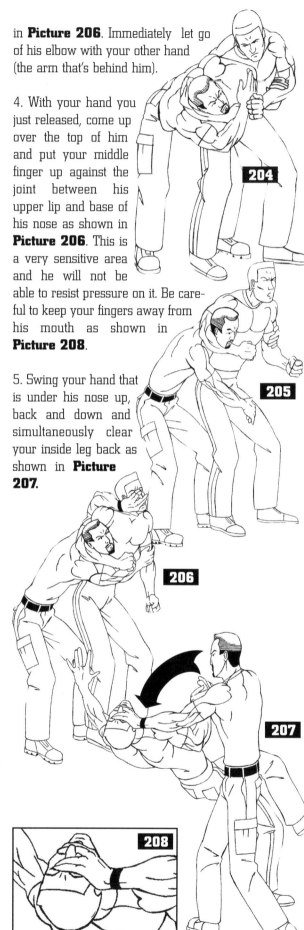

either from the outside as shown in **Picture 203** or inside as shown in **Picture 204** closeup if he is too big to get all the way around. This neutralizes his free arm.

3. Hit him in the groin with your free hand in **Picture 205**. Then grab his hand which elbow you are securing with your free hand, press it against him as shown

in **Picture 206**. Immediately let go of his elbow with your other hand (the arm that's behind him).

4. With your hand you just released, come up over the top of him and put your middle finger up against the joint between his upper lip and base of his nose as shown in **Picture 206**. This is a very sensitive area and he will not be able to resist pressure on it. Be careful to keep your fingers away from his mouth as shown in **Picture 208**.

5. Swing your hand that is under his nose up, back and down and simultaneously clear your inside leg back as shown in **Picture 207**.

6. You can either:

   a. 'Stretch him out' as shown in **Picture 209, 210, 211, and 212** and kick him in the back (kidney) or head as necessary or

b. Drop a knee on his ribs and hit the area below his ear (or head if necessary) as shown in **Picture 213 and 214** and if necessary stretch him out and follow up with kicks or hit him until you are confident that he is no longer a threat.

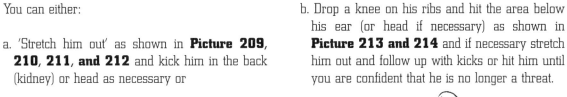

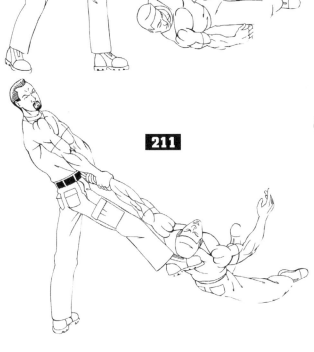

7. Stretching him out means pulling his arm hard enough to drag him. You should be above his shoulder-line. This minimizes his ability to regain control.

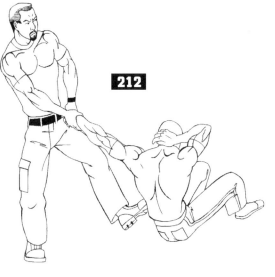

Headlocks - Side Headlock - Low Position

REFERENCE

Video Tape: **3**
Section: **5.0**

DVD: **2**
Volume: **2**
Menu Chapter: **5**
Section: **5.0**

SIDE HEADLOCK – LOW POSITION
Primary Danger – His Free Hand

1. You are being held as shown in **Picture 215**. Remember, even though there may be pressure on your throat and he may be squeezing hard enough to restrict your air supply or blood flow, that is not the primary danger. His free hand can cause enough damage to render you ineffective, by punching you repeatedly in the face. That is the primary danger. Despite the discomfort, don't panic. You have time to break his hold, but you must act quickly. First you must neutralize his free hand.

2. Because he is bending you down the previous technique will not work effectively.

3. Put your opposite side hand between his hand and your face as shown in **Picture 216**. At the same time, with your other hand, reach around his back and secure his elbow either from the outside as shown in **Picture 216** or inside as shown in **Picture 217** if he is too big to get all the way around. This neutralizes his free arm.

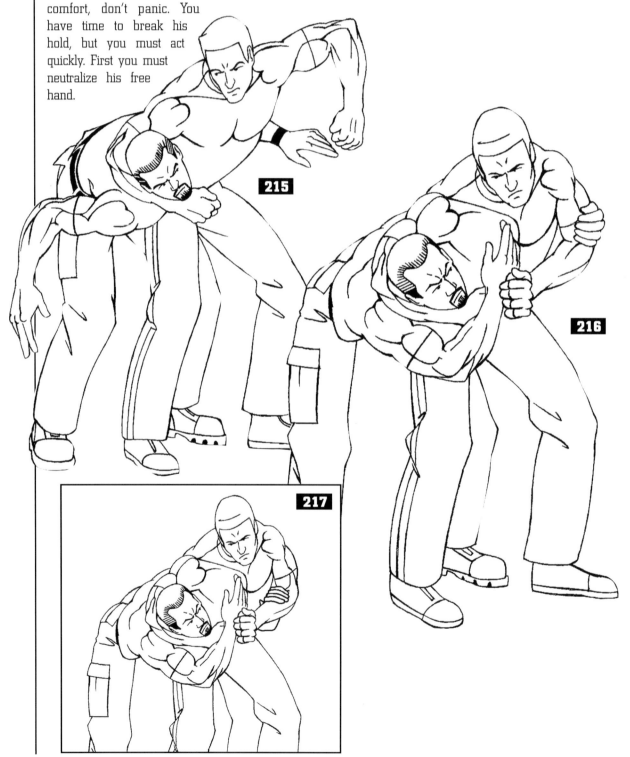

215

216

217

4. With your free hand, form a 'V' between your thumb and the side of your hand as shown in **Picture 218**

and push his knee from behind straight down in front of the **center** of his body as shown in **Picture 219**. The push is a hard driving hit behind the knee joint as though you are pushing through the knee. The impact will damage his knee if it hits a hard surface. His heel should be pointing up if you pushed the knee in the proper direction.

5. Drop your knee down onto the back of his ankle as shown in **Picture 220** to break it and escape his grasp which will have loosened or released. Alternatively, you can strike down hard on the back of his ankle with your hand for the same effect. Restraining or termination options are also available.

6. As you exit, if necessary you can elbow strike the back as shown in **Picture 220**.

**F.I.G.H.T. Tip:
Positioning**
When you push his knee forward, you are pushing it diagonally toward a point in front of the center of his body.

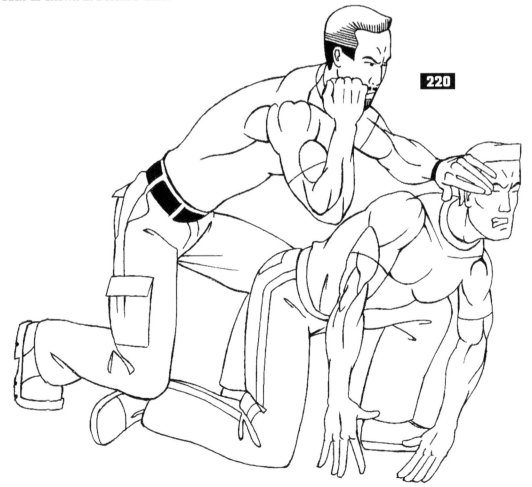

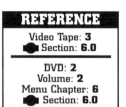

REFERENCE
Video Tape: **3**
◆ Section: **6.0**

DVD: **2**
Volume: **2**
Menu Chapter: **6**
◆ Section: **6.0**

**F.I.G.H.T. Tip:
Alternate Technique**
The technique for a Rear Headlock-Pulling also works on the Rear Headlock-Static. If you find it difficult to effectively perform this technique on much larger opponents even after properly practicing it you can rely on that technique.

REAR HEADLOCK- STATIC
Primary Danger- His Arm Choking You

1. You are being held from behind as shown in **Picture 221**. You are not being pulled backwards yet. You must immediately take pressure off of your throat to prevent being choked-out relatively quickly.

2. Hook his arm and pull it down as shown in **Picture 222** digging your chin in behind it. This will remove some pressure from your throat and buy a bit of time.

3. Base yourself as shown in **Picture 222** by simultaneously widening your legs, thereby dropping down slightly, leaning forward slightly and lowering your hips. This is a movement that will be used in other techniques. Maintain your hold on your attacker's arm.

4. Lean forward as shown in **Picture 223**. Do not try to pick up your attacker, if he is too big or you lack strength you won't be able to. Rather, you are **leaning** forward and curving his body. This requires little strength regardless of relative size, and will cause him to stand more on his toes as shown, making him lighter.

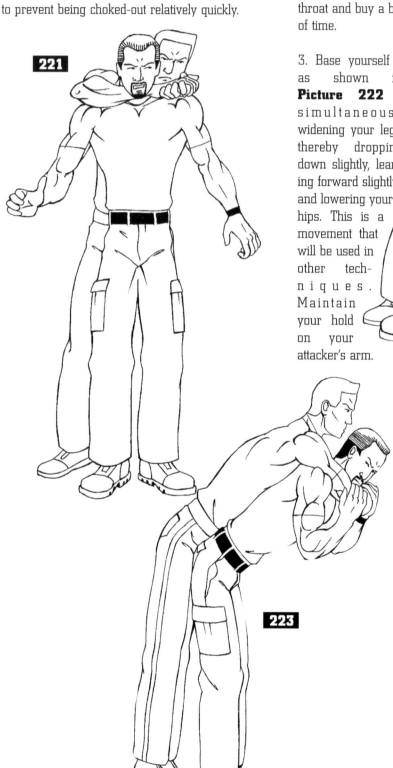

will appear as though you are trying to touch your forehead to your knee opposite the side you are throwing him over. This will cause him to fall forward and to the side, over your shoulder. Maintain your grip on his arm. Do not disconnect.

6. You can either:
a. 'Stretch him out' as shown in **Picture 225**, **226**, **227**, **and 228** and kick him in the back (kidney) or head as necessary or

b. Drop knee on his ribs and hit the area below his ear (or head if necessary) as shown in **Picture 229 and 230** and if necessary stretch him out and follow up with kicks or hit him until you are sure he is no longer a threat.

7. The keys to this technique working against a larger opponent are proper basing, leaning forward rather than picking up the attacker, and a smooth strong turn down towards the knee. If done properly a much smaller person can throw a much larger one to the ground.

5. Once he is on his toes you will throw him. Do so by bending forward and simultaneously twisting your body **away from the elbow that is holding your neck**, as shown in picture **Picture 224**. The motion

REFERENCE

Video Tape: **3**
◆ Section: **7.0**

DVD: **2**
Volume: **2**
Menu Chapter: **7**
◆ Section: **7.0**

REAR HEADLOCK- PULLING

Primary Danger- Loss of Balance

1. You are being held from behind as shown in **Picture 231**. You are being pulled backwards. You must immediately regain your balance. He may throw you down to the ground (bad), or take you to a secondary location or do worse.

2. Step firmly back with the leg on the same side he grabbed you from (to 7 o'clock if your left leg, or to 5 o'clock if your right leg). Step outside of, and behind, your attacker's foot.

**F.I.G.H.T. Tip:
Alternate Technique**
The technique for a Rear Headlock-Pulling also works on the Rear Headlock- Static. If you find it difficult to effectively perform this technique on much larger opponents even after properly practicing it you can rely on that technique.

3. Simultaneously hook his arm with your hands as shown in **Picture 232** and pull down to release pressure.

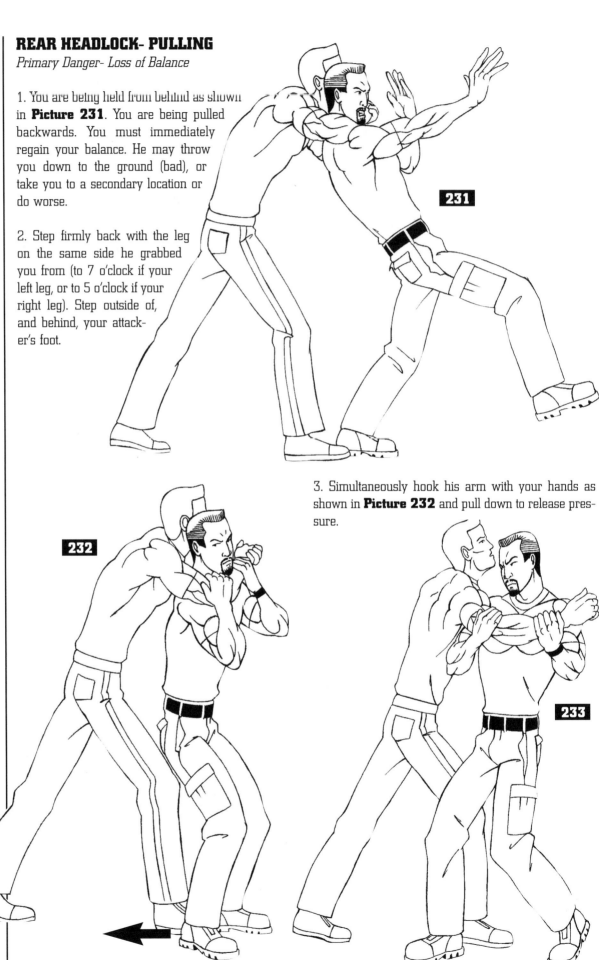

4. Swing the leg that you didn't step back, and wrap all the way around so that you face the opposite direction as shown in **Picture 233**. Note that as you swing your leg your foot travels slightly beyond parallel with your other foot. Maintain your grip and stay tight against his body, thigh on thigh. Push your shoulder into him to put him on his heels.

5. Quickly elbow his side with your inside arm and regain your grip of his arm with it immediately.

6. Maintaining your grip on his arm, slam him down by yanking him toward you and downward while turning your body away from him and bumping him forward with your shoulder as shown in **Picture 234**. The combination of all of those forces in the forward and downward direction will make the throw work. Do it violently, and if he struggles, hit him again with your elbow to loosen him up.

7. You can either:
    a. 'Stretch him out' as shown in **Picture 235, 236, 237, and 238** and kick him in the back (kidney) or head as necessary or

    b. Drop a knee on his ribs and hit the area below his ear (or head if necessary) as shown in **Picture 239 and 240** and if necessary stretch him out and follow up with kicks.

REFERENCE
Video Tape: **3**
◆ Section: **8.0**

DVD: **2**
Volume: **2**
Menu Chapter: **8**
◆ Section: **8.0**

REFERENCE
Video Tape: **3**
◆ Section: **9.0**

DVD: **2**
Volume: **2**
Menu Chapter: **9**
◆ Section: **9.0**

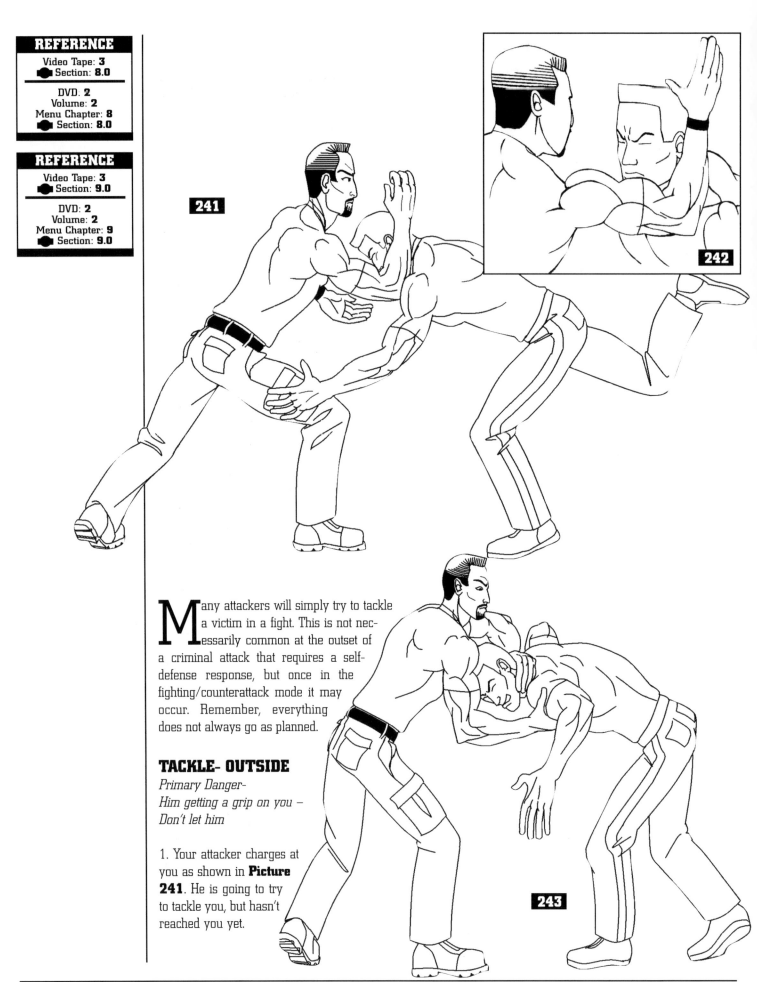

Many attackers will simply try to tackle a victim in a fight. This is not necessarily common at the outset of a criminal attack that requires a self-defense response, but once in the fighting/counterattack mode it may occur. Remember, everything does not always go as planned.

TACKLE- OUTSIDE

Primary Danger-
Him getting a grip on you –
Don't let him

1. Your attacker charges at you as shown in **Picture 241**. He is going to try to tackle you, but hasn't reached you yet.

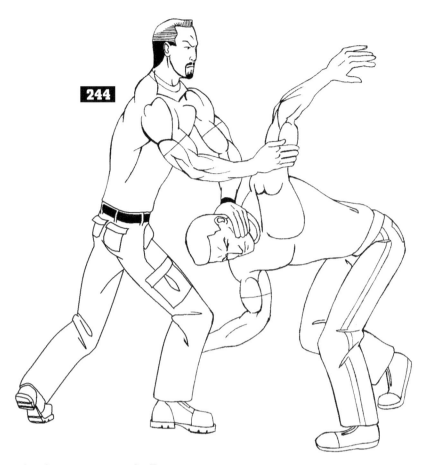

244

2. Step forward with your **strong side**. Put your strong arm directly in front of you, bent 90 degrees. Lean into the position as shown in **Picture 241**.

3. Let your attacker run into your forearm with his collar bone (or head – don't aim). This may hurt your forearm, but it will hurt him also. **Picture 242**.

4. Immediately slide your hand under his arm near the armpit as shown in **Picture 243**. If you ended up hitting his collarbone on the other side of his neck, slide your hand over the back of his neck and under his arm near the armpit.

245

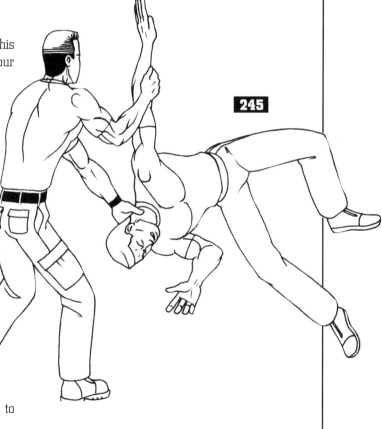

5. Pull up and across with the hand under his arm while pushing down and through on his opposite shoulder-blade with your other hand as shown in **Picture 244**. Simultaneously swing your rear leg behind you while pivoting on your front foot and rotating your chest to the opposite direction. As shown in **Picture 245**. This will throw him to the ground and his momentum will cause him to roll past you.

6. Step back and escape if possible or reposition to attack if he gets up.

REFERENCE

Video Tape: **3**
◆ Section: **10.0**

DVD: **2**
Volume: **2**
Menu Chapter: **10**
◆ Section: **10.0**

TACKLE - INSIDE

Primary Danger- Him taking you to the ground and dominating you

1. Your attacker charges at you as shown in **Picture 246**. He is trying to tackle you, and unfortunately he gets his arms around you. It is too late to avoid going to the ground, so instead you will avoid being in an inferior position when you get there.

2. You are going to essentially SIT DOWN as shown in **Picture 247**.

3. In the process of sitting, hook your strong side leg inside the attacker's left leg as shown clearly in **Picture 248**.

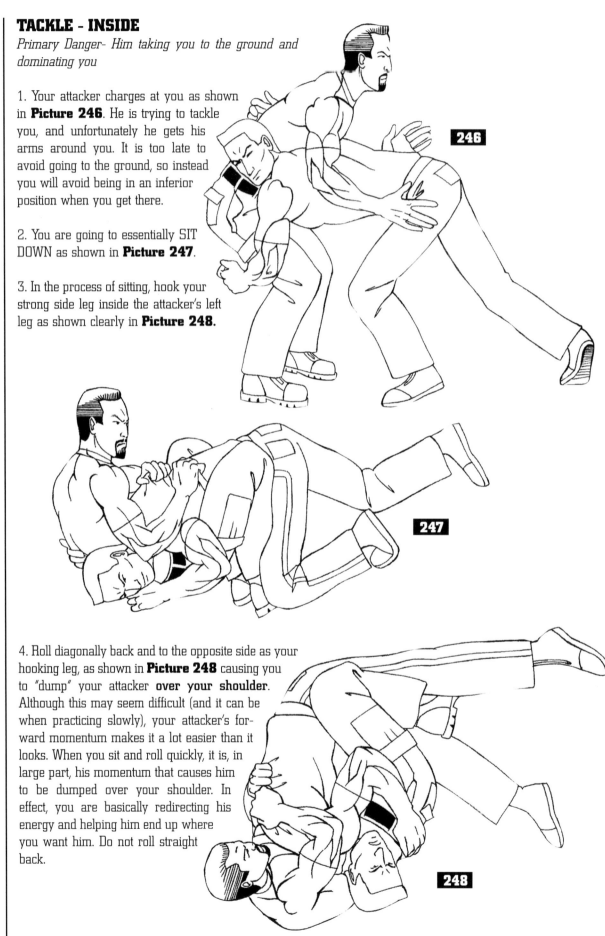

4. Roll diagonally back and to the opposite side as your hooking leg, as shown in **Picture 248** causing you to "dump" your attacker **over your shoulder**. Although this may seem difficult (and it can be when practicing slowly), your attacker's forward momentum makes it a lot easier than it looks. When you sit and roll quickly, it is, in large part, his momentum that causes him to be dumped over your shoulder. In effect, you are basically redirecting his energy and helping him end up where you want him. Do not roll straight back.

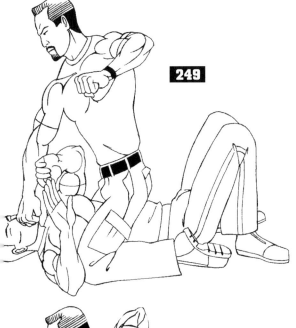

5. Your goal is to end up mounted on him as shown in **Picture 249**. Note that your knees are outside his sides tightly up against him and your feet are pointing backward.

6. Immediately punch him in the face a couple of times, deliver an elbow and if necessary smash his head into the ground (dangerous - use in case of extreme threat to your safety) or, if he is sufficiently debilitated already, get up as shown in **Pictures 250, 251, and 252**. Always try to exit to one of his sides to avoid his arms or legs trapping you. Also, if he is covering up when you deliver your 2 punch combination, reach under his arms and "strip" them away to expose his face for the elbow.

F.I.G.H.T. Tip: Positioning

Note that when in the mount position the defender's feet are pointed backward and are tight against the attacker's body. This is an important tactic for reasons that will be covered in the ground survival series.

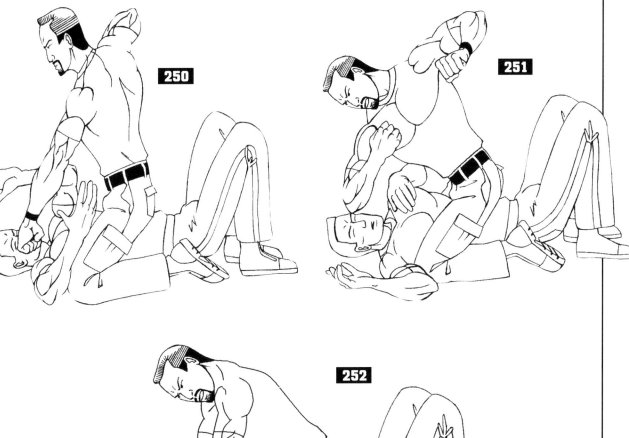

Knife Threat Defenses

REFERENCE

Video Tape: **4**
Section: **1.0-6.0**

DVD: **3**
Volume: **1**
Menu Chapter: **1-6**
Section: **1.0-6.0**

Similar to assaults involving a gun, a violent encounter with a knife-wielding assailant is extremely stressful. In many ways encountering an attacker who is flailing away at you with a knife or who is threatening with a knife is even more stressful than encountering one with a gun. The reason is simple. In an encounter with someone with a gun, if you remain composed and act quickly and effectively when the time comes, you stand a very good chance of not being shot. Conversely, if you do all of the same in an encounter with a knife armed assailant, you nonetheless stand a very good chance of actually getting cut.

The reasons:

- According to several studies of violent encounters involving knives, about 75% of the time the victims did not even realize a knife was involved and that they had been cut until after the attack was over. Knives are hard to see, they are silent and they are easily deployed in very close quarters combat. You may be doing everything right, and still be cut

- Even if you are able to detect that a knife is present, the knife is essentially an extension of the hand it is in. Where the hand goes, so goes the knife. A gun really has a very limited effective range of operation. Part of your body has to be in the line of fire extending straight from the barrel for you to get hit. If the side or top or bottom of the gun itself hits you lightly, no big deal. With the knife, if the hand is near you the knife might poke you, or slice into you. It might have edges on both sides. Even if it touches you ineffectively it is a mere fraction of an inch rotation that makes it effective. In fact, it is as likely that the knife will cut you as it is that the attacker's hand will touch you - a very likely occurrence.

- Skilled knife fighters use very fast, very tight motions that are hard to detect and even harder to effectively block or seize.

The techniques that follow deal with two aspects of knife encounters – threats where the person is holding the knife stationary and has a demand, and attacks where the person is swinging or thrusting the knife attempting to stab or slash you. Because of the difficulty of dealing with a knife in motion, while we teach empty hand techniques against the knife, we encourage you to carry a folding knife with you consistent with whatever is permitted by local or other applicable law.

It is the F.I.G.H.T. and Haganah philosophy that when attacked with a knife you should deploy a weapon. This levels the playing field so to speak, both physically and psychologically, and may dissuade an attacker from continuing to press his attack.. If you do decide to carry a knife, we encourage you to take our Israeli Tactical Knife fighting series to learn to properly fight knife versus knife. It is available on video or DVD at *www.fight2survive.com*. If you do not carry a knife, or if you are in a situation where you are confronted by a knife attack and cannot be armed, you will have to be very effective at empty hand techniques.

There are certain basic components associated with knife attacks :

- Slashes and stabs are the two distinct types of attacking motions. In a slash, the attacker is swinging the knife (even if a very short distance) in an attempt to cut you. In a stab, he is trying to stick the knife into you. In reality most attacks involve a combination of these motions, such as slash and stab, stab and slash, slash only and stab only, and these combinations may occur in repeated random order.

- Angles of attack. There are nine general angles (including straight) along which an attacking motion might come, as shown below. In reality most attacks will involve a combination of these general angles in conjunction with a combination of slashes and stabs. **DIA. 2**

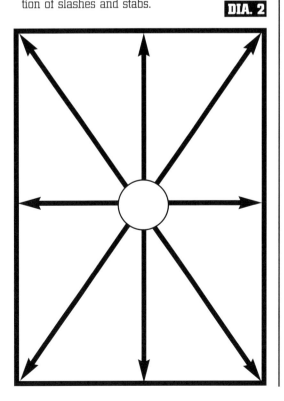

- Footwork. Generally, your attacker will be moving as he slashes or stabs.

There are some common elements to all empty hand defenses against a knife attack:

- Maintaining your distance until you are ready to enter, or escape if possible.

- Identifying the angle of attack. It is hard enough to identify the angle that the knife is coming from, let alone whether it is a stab or slash. These defenses are designed to minimize the need for differentiating between a stab and slash by concentrating on the angle of attack. Unless otherwise noted, they work equally well against both stabs and slashes.

- Angling up. Footwork that moves you out of the knife's trajectory is a key element of every technique where you are not being held. It is paramount to combine proper footwork with all knife defenses; this is especially important during your entry, in order to safely get out of the way in the event you miss your target. We will use the clock concept to describe your footwork to refresh your memory.

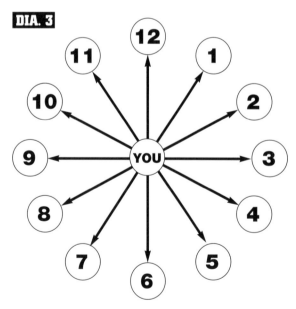

DIA. 3

- Entering with a seizing of the knife arm, or in some circumstances a block or check followed by seizing or securing.

- Maintaining contact with the knife arm/hand. Once you make contact with the knife arm/hand on entry, you never lose contact. The attacker

will try to pull the knife free. You don't want this to happen, and the last thing you want to do unless you can clearly flee the scene safely is disconnect from him. This would allow him to attack again.

- Incapacitating or terminating the attacker. A knife is a deadly weapon and an attacker with a knife has the potential to kill you. You must eliminate his ability to cause you serious injury or death in whatever manner you believe under the circumstances is reasonable and necessary. Do not give him a second chance.

90 DEGREE BLOCKS REVIEW

Certain of the empty hand defenses involve blocking the knife arm or checking the knife arm. A block stops the motion of the arm. A check allows the motion to continue in its original direction, but protects against a change in direction of the arm. In either case, as we discussed in the Concepts and Terminology portion of this manual, your blocking (or checking) arm must be bent at the elbow 90 degrees. This creates a firm block or check with your forearm that will not easily collapse under force and that also will not easily allow the attackers arm to slip. This is especially important in the case of knife defenses that use this technique because the attacker is holding a knife so if your block or check allows his arm to slip you may be directing the knife toward your body.

SEIZING OR SECURING THE KNIFE ARM

Whenever a technique requires the seizing or securing of the attacker's knife arm, it will use the battery concept. That is – an under (+) and over (-) grip. It will also require you to pin the arm to you or your attacker, maintaining at least two points of contact. This approach is critical to the integrity of the knife defense. Once you capture his weapon arm, he will put much effort into trying to free it. Any technique that allows for a single hand grip on the arm without the arm also being pinned to either his or your body is inherently weak. The attacker will yank the knife free and you will be dealing with an escalating attack.

OVERHEAD STAB (ICE PICK STYLE)
Late or Early Identification of Attack
Non-Lethal Response
Primary Danger – Knife Line of Travel

1. The attacker is swinging the knife at you from overhead typically in a stabbing motion, as shown in **Picture 253**, but possibly in a slashing motion. Both are treated the same way. If you identified the attack late, you will flow into this from an instinctive reaction. If you identified the attack early but want to avoid lethal force, this technique works.

2. Step in, duck down and block the knife arm with same side arm as the knife is coming from bent 90 degrees as shown in **Picture 254**. You probably will flinch and block instinctively, so all you are programming at this point is the recognition of the angle and always bending the arm 90 degrees on the block. The 90 degree angle of your arm is important to create a secure block.

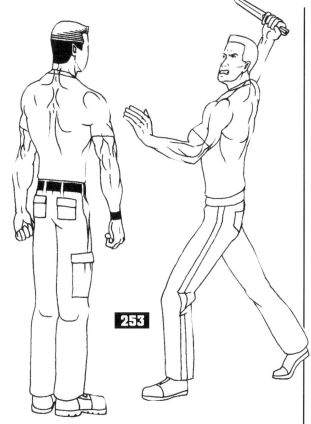

253

254

3. Shoot your other arm inside his knife arm at the elbow joint as shown in **Picture 254**.

4. Simultaneously, push in toward him on the blocking arm while sliding your hand to about his wrist to cup it, and grab your forearm with your other hand as shown in **Picture 255**.

5. Step through with your inside leg as shown in **Picture 256** and simultaneously forcefully twist his arm backward as shown. You are pushing inward and backward. This will incapacitate the arm by either breaking the forearm bone or ripping his shoulder out of the socket, causing him to drop the knife. You can also throw him to the ground by continuing your forward motion and pushing down toward your center-line.

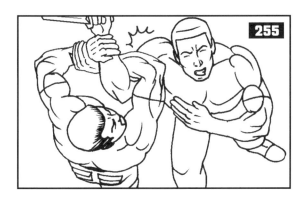

255

256

REFERENCE
Video Tape: **4**
Section: **11.3**
DVD: **3**
Volume: **1**
Menu Chapter: **11**
Section: **11.3**

Overhead Stab (Ice Pick Style) - Lethal Response

REFERENCE
Video Tape: **4**
● Section: **11.0**

DVD: **3**
Volume: **1**
Menu Chapter: **11**
● Section: **11.0**

OVERHEAD STAB (ICE PICK STYLE)
Early Identification of Attack -Lethal Response
Primary Danger – Knife Line of Travel

1. The attacker is swinging the knife at you from overhead as shown in **Picture 257**. This type of attack is not designed to scare you; it is designed to kill you.

2. Step to 11 o'clock and shoot both hands up as shown in **Picture 258**. This will direct his knife arm past you.

3. Borrow his momentum to sweep his knife arm into his body with a curved motion using both of your arms. Push against him pinning the knife arm to him using your inside arm and hand as shown in **Picture 259**.

4. Using your outside hand, push his chin away from you as shown in **Pictures 260 and 261**. This is done rapidly and forcefully to keep him distracted and to likely cause him to push his head and body toward you, further securing your position and giving you momentum for your objective.

5. To incapacitate him, take him down by pushing behind his knee with your foot while simultaneously pushing his body forward with yours. Then, step on the ankle to break or severely damage it.

6. To terminate him if necessary, reverse the pushing motion against his chin and snap his head back toward you and upward in a diagonal motion as shown in **Picture 262**.

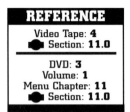

7. If the attacker is swinging the knife with his opposite hand, you will end up in a somewhat more rear position. Practice this to get comfortable. Also, if you are left-handed you can step to 1 o'clock. However, while that will allow you to use your strong arm for the head control it will put you in the more rearward position (in some ways less secure) against right handed attackers (most common). Finally, if you identify that the attack is coming from the left hand versus right, you can step to 1 o'clock instead of 11 o'clock, but it increases your programming time. Again, practice variations to get comfortable. Most people stick with training the basic approach- it is more likely to work under the pressure of the attack.

F.I.G.H.T. Tip: Positioning
The counterattack position you are in after passing the knife relies on a combination of your attacker's forward momentum, you pushing into him and your inside leg being behind him for its strength. Move quickly or he may disconnect.

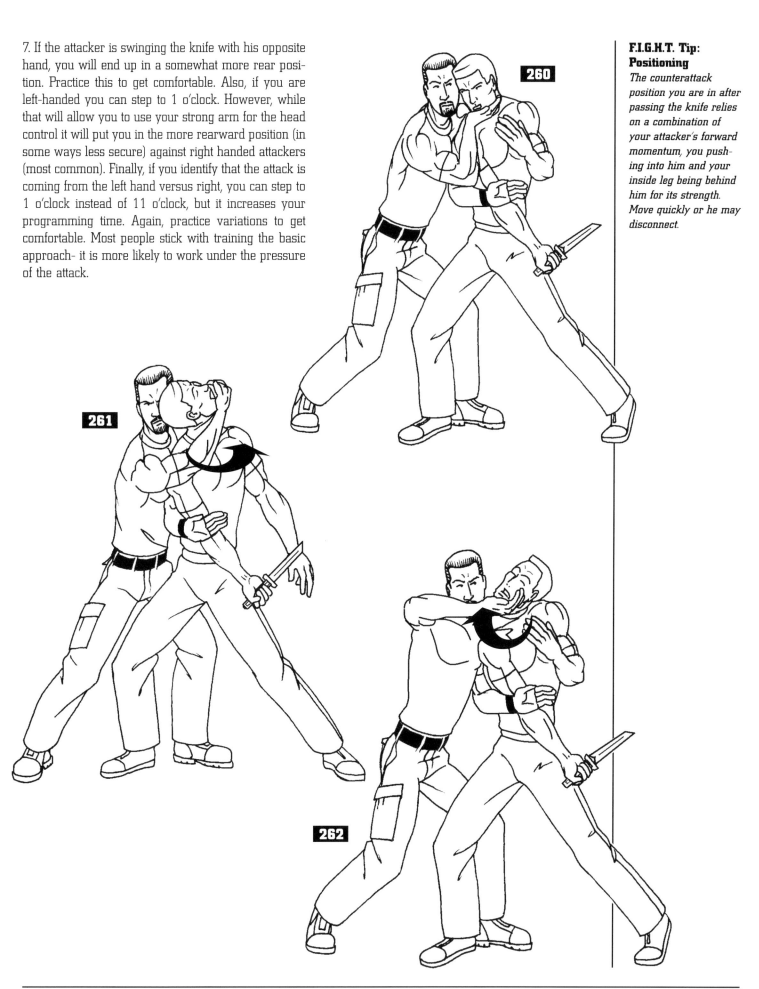

Stab/Slash From Upper Left to Right (Attacker's Right to Left)

REFERENCE
Video Tape: **4**
Section: **7.0**

DVD: **3**
Volume: **1**
Menu Chapter: **7**
Section: **7.0**

STAB/SLASH FROM YOUR UPPER LEFT TO RIGHT

(Attacker's Right to Left)
Primary Danger – Knife Line of Travel

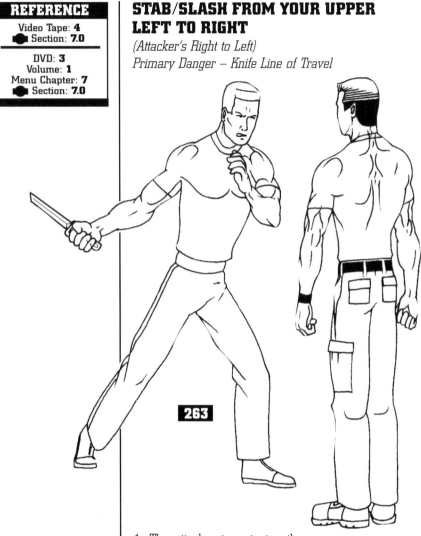

1. The attacker is swinging the knife at you on your left side from higher to lower as shown in **Picture 263**. It doesn't matter whether it is a stab or slash, what his grip is or which hand he is using to hold the knife. You won't have time to identify both the angle of attack and the type of strike.

2. Angle up and grab the knife arm on the forearm near the wrist with your hands as shown in **Picture 264**. The angle up is accomplished by moving both feet to 2 o'clock. This helps you stay away from the knife. The grab is done with one hand facing up and one hand facing down as shown in **Picture 265**, the Battery Concept. Either hand can face either way. This creates a secure grip. Practice this repeatedly. Also, note that the arms are not bent. Bent arms may collapse on impact or be too close, both bringing the knife into you.

3. Pull (yank) him toward you and down and kick to the groin area as shown in **Picture 266**. It is important that you yank him because his first reaction to your seizing is likely to pull away. If your raise your leg to kick and he pulls away, you will be off balance giving him a momentary advantage. Pulling him offsets that.

Stab/Slash From Upper Left to Right (Attacker's Right to Left)

Upon completing the kick, be sure to bring your leg back to its original position.

4. Immediately after the groin kick, if you end up on the outside (if he held the knife left handed):

   a. Pass the knife to your right side as shown in **Picture 267**. This is accomplished by swinging his arm in front of you with your inside hand and scooping under it with your outside hand as shown in **Picture 268**. Do NOT step forward until the knife passes you. Then continue with step 5.

IMPORTANT NOTE:

For purposes of illustration, we have rotated Picture 268 to re-position the "Good Guy" facing you.

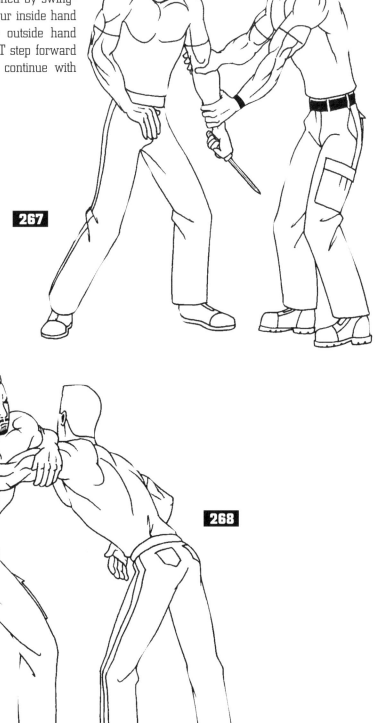

267

268

Stab/Slash From Upper Left to Right (Attacker's Right to Left)

5. Immediately after the groin kick if you end up on the inside or immediately after step 4 if you were on the outside:

    a. Step in as shown in **Picture 269**, and

    b. Secure his knife arm to you as shown in **Picture 269**. You are hugging his arm to you tightly from underneath with your outside arm while gripping his armpit with your inside hand from over the top and pinning his shoulder to you. One up, one down- battery concept. Hold tightly and you are very secure.

F.I.G.H.T. Tip: Positioning

You can end up on the outside in any of the angled (side to side) knife attacks as a result of the hand which the attacker uses to hold the knife. This requires that you become proficient in moving the knife arm to achieve a point of reference from each position. Practice with your training partner using each hand.

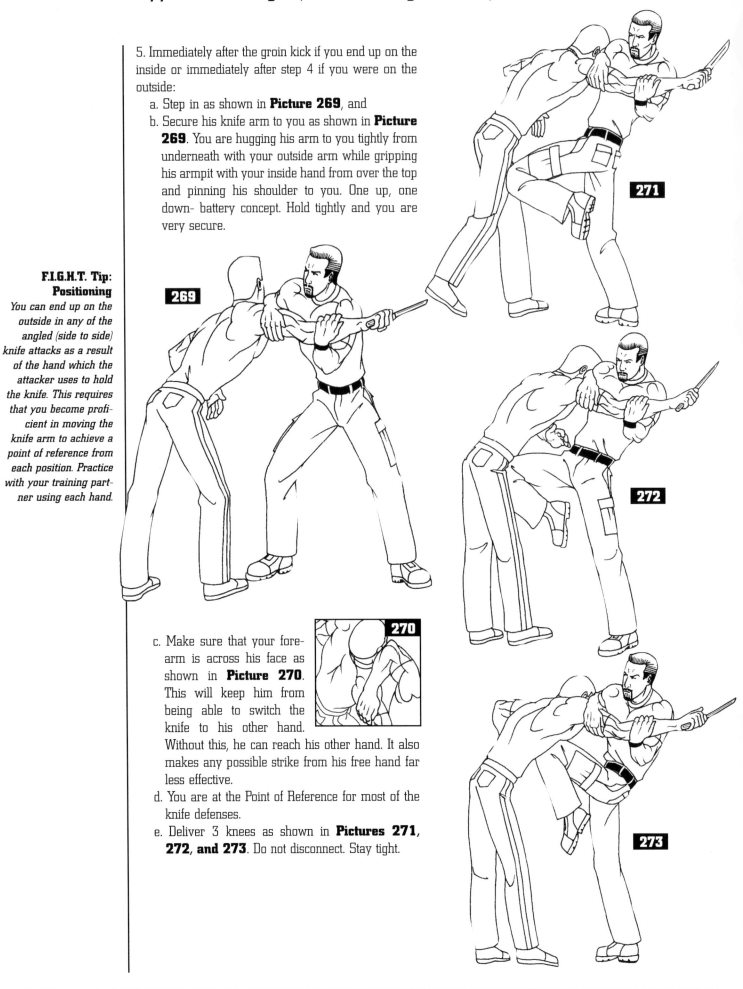

    c. Make sure that your forearm is across his face as shown in **Picture 270**. This will keep him from being able to switch the knife to his other hand. Without this, he can reach his other hand. It also makes any possible strike from his free hand far less effective.

    d. You are at the Point of Reference for most of the knife defenses.

    e. Deliver 3 knees as shown in **Pictures 271, 272, and 273**. Do not disconnect. Stay tight.

Stab/Slash From Upper Left to Right (Attacker's Right to Left)

f. Choose your objective:

Restrain and Disarm

(only recommended for law enforcement)

1. All disarms are done from a takedown
2. Push straight down on his neck (piston motion) to 6 o'clock as shown in **Picture 274 and 275**. Do not let go of his knife arm. He should be dropped right in front of you.
3. Drop down on his body with a knee and apply pressure to his neck with a knee as shown in picture **Picture 276**. Hit him if necessary.
4. Either strip the knife as shown in **Picture Series 277** or peel the knife out of his hand as shown in **Picture Series 278**. Peeling is the preferred method, and is done by squeezing his fingers closed by pressing on the finger nails and bending the wrist inward to create pain and then digging your fingers under the knife handle and rolling his hand open.

Incapacitate

1. Step on the forward foot as shown in **Picture 279**
2. Violently push away from you to break the ankle as shown in **Picture 280**. Push forward and toward the side holding the knife to avoid the knife whipping into you.

Terminate

1. Slide your inside hand down his neck to his chin as shown in **Picture 281**. Stay tight. It can increase effectiveness to push his chin toward your body before wrenching.
2. Wrench violently up and back at an angle as shown in **Picture 282**.

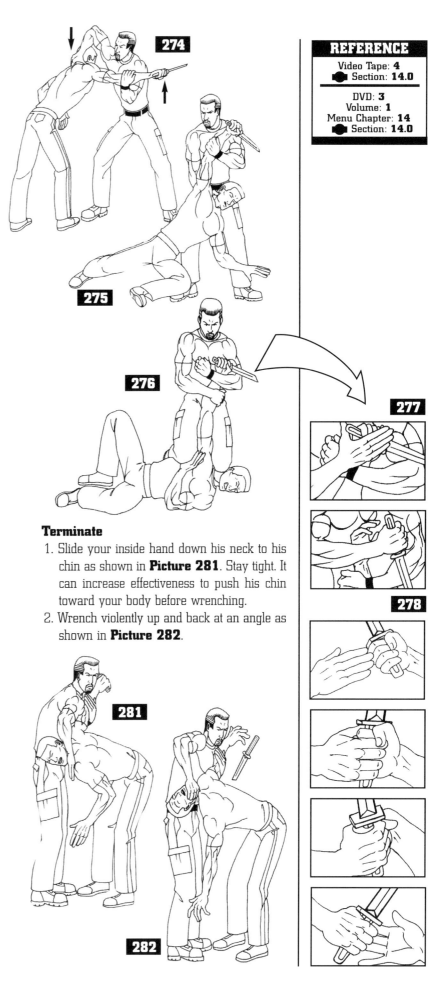

REFERENCE

Video Tape: **4**
Section: **14.0**

DVD: **3**
Volume: **1**
Menu Chapter: **14**
Section: **14.0**

Stab/Slash From Your Upper Right to Left (Attacker's Left to Right)

REFERENCE
Video Tape: **4**
Section: **8.0**

DVD: **3**
Volume: **1**
Menu Chapter: **8**
Section: **8.0**

STAB/SLASH FROM YOUR UPPER RIGHT TO LEFT

(Attacker's Left to right)
Primary Danger – Knife Line of Travel

1. The attacker is swinging the knife at you on your right side from higher to lower as shown in **Picture 283**. It doesn't matter whether it is a stab or slash, what his grip is or which hand he is using to hold the knife. You won't have time to identify both the angle of attack and the type of strike.

2. Angle up and grab the knife arm on the forearm near the wrist with your hands as shown in **Picture 284**. The angle up is accomplished by moving both feet to 10 o'clock. This helps you stay away from the knife. The grab is done with one hand facing up and one hand facing down as shown in **Picture 285**, which also shows your relative position. Either hand can face either way. This creates a secure grip. Practice this repeatedly. Also, note that the arms are not bent. Bent arms may collapse on impact or be too close, both may bring the knife into you.

F.I.G.H.T. Tip: Positioning
You can end up on the outside in any of the angled (side to side) knife attacks as a result of the hand which the attacker uses to hold the knife. This requires that you become proficient in moving the knife arm to achieve a point of reference from each position. Practice with your training partner using each hand.

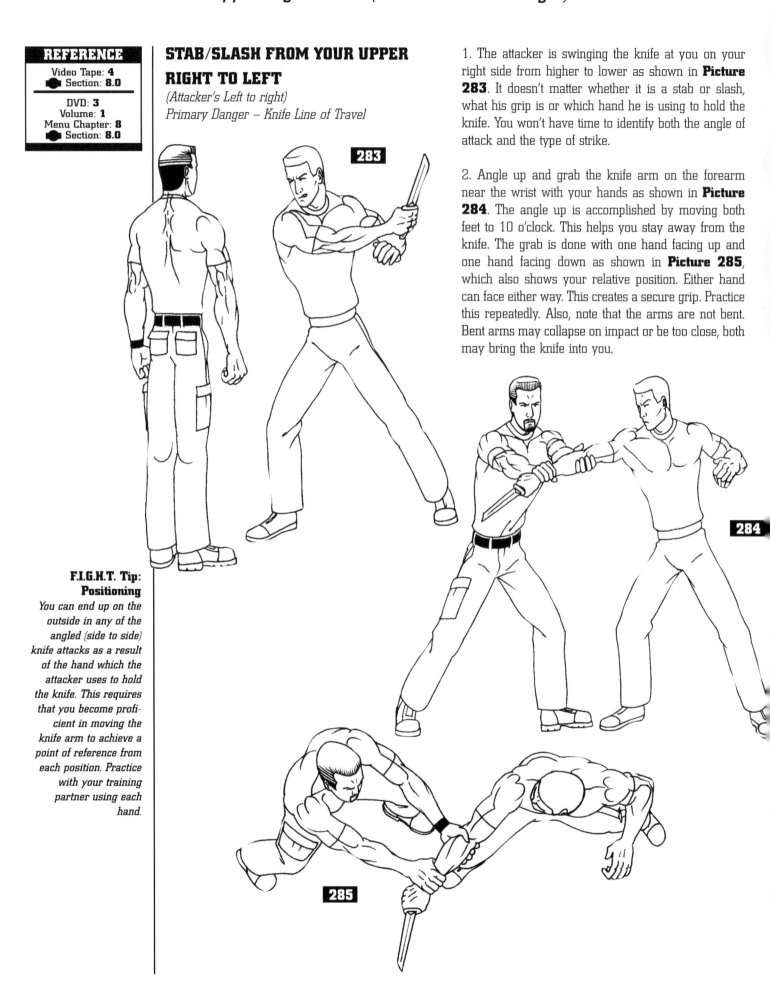

Stab/Slash From Your Upper Right to Left (Attacker's Left to Right)

3. Pull (yank) him toward you and down and kick to the groin area as shown in **Picture 286**. It is important that you yank him because his first reaction to your seizing is likely to pull away. If your raise your leg to kick and he pulls away, you will be off balance giving him a momentary advantage. Pulling him offsets that. Upon completing the kick, be sure to bring your leg back to its original position.

4. Immediately after the groin kick, if you end up on the outside (he has the knife in his right hand):

a. Pass the knife to your left side as shown in **Picture 287**. This is accomplished by swinging his arm in front of you with your inside hand and scooping under it with your outside hand as shown in **Picture 288**. Do NOT step forward until the knife passes you. Then continue with step 5.

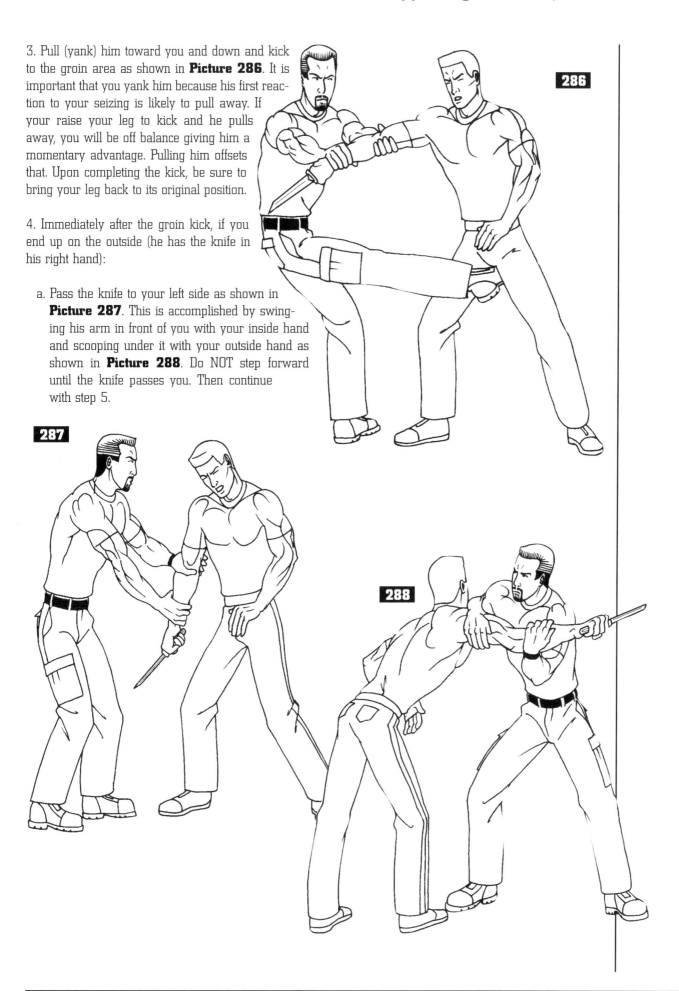

Stab/Slash From Your Upper Right to Left (Attacker's Left to Right)

5. Immediately after the groin kick if you end up on the inside or immediately after step 4 if you were on the outside:

a. Step in as shown in **Picture 289**, and

b. Secure his knife arm to you as shown in **Picture 289**. You are hugging his arm to you tightly from underneath with your outside arm while gripping his armpit with your inside hand from over the top and pinning his shoulder to you. One up, one down- battery concept. Hold tightly and you are very secure.

c. Make sure that your forearm is across his face as shown in **Picture 290**. This will keep him from being able to switch the knife to his other hand. Without this, he can reach his other hand. It also makes any possible strike from his free hand far less effective.

d. You are at your Point of Reference for most of the knife defenses.

e. Deliver 3 knees as shown in **Picture 291, 292 and 293**. Do not disconnect. Stay tight.

Stab/Slash From Your Upper Right to Left (Attacker's Left to Right)

f. Choose your objective:

Restrain and Disarm

(only recommended for law enforcement)

1. All disarms are done from a takedown
2. Push straight down on his neck (piston motion) to 6 o'clock as shown in **Picture 294 and 295**. Do not let go of his knife arm. He should be dropped right in front of you.
3. Drop down on his body with a knee and apply pressure to his neck with a knee as shown in picture **Picture 296**. Hit him if necessary.
4. Either strip the knife as shown in **Picture 297** or peel the knife out of his hand as shown in **Picture 298**. Peeling is the preferred method, and is done by squeezing his fingers closed by pressing on the finger nails to create pain and then digging your fingers under the knife handle and rolling his hand open

Incapacitate

1. Step on the forward foot as shown in **Picture 299**
2. Violently push away from you to break the ankle as shown in **Picture 300**. Push forward and toward the side holding the knife to avoid the knife whipping into you.

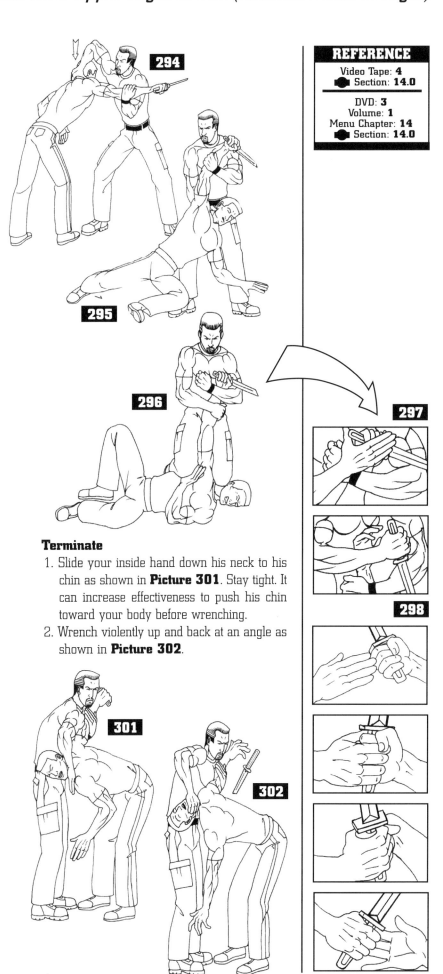

Terminate

1. Slide your inside hand down his neck to his chin as shown in **Picture 301**. Stay tight. It can increase effectiveness to push his chin toward your body before wrenching.
2. Wrench violently up and back at an angle as shown in **Picture 302**.

REFERENCE

Video Tape: **4**
Section: **14.0**

DVD: **3**
Volume: **1**
Menu Chapter: **14**
Section: **14.0**

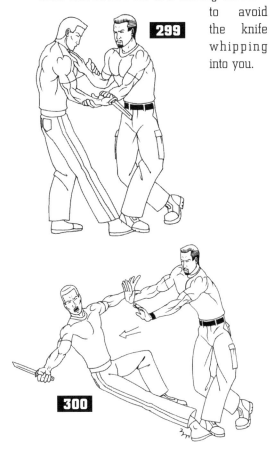

Knife Threat Defenses

Stab/Slash - Side to Side; Lower Right or Left Traveling Upward; Straight Stab

REFERENCE
Video Tape: **4**
◖▬ Section: **9.0-10.0**

DVD: **3**
Volume: **1**
Menu Chapter: **9-10**
◖▬ Section: **9.0-10.0**

REFERENCE
Video Tape: **4**
◖▬ Section: **12.0**

DVD: **3**
Volume: **1**
Menu Chapter: **12**
◖▬ Section: **12.0**

STAB/ SLASH - SIDE TO SIDE

Primary Danger – Knife Line of Travel

The defense against attacks running horizontally is the same as the corresponding defenses for Upper Right to Left or vice versa (depending upon which side of you the attack originates from).

STAB/SLASH- LOWER RIGHT OR LEFT TRAVELING UPWARD

Primary Danger – Knife Line of Travel

The defense against an angled attack moving from low to high can also be the same as the corresponding defense for Upper Right to Left or vice versa (depending upon which side of you the attack originates from). However, low to high attacks can also be treated the same as underhand stabs as described below.

STRAIGHT STAB

Primary Danger – Knife Line of Travel

1. The attacker is thrusting he knife at you straight on as shown in **Picture 303**. As with all straight on attacks, the primary danger is that you are in the line of fire. Therefore moving out of it is your first goal.

2. Move to 11 o'clock and at the same time check with your left arm (bent 90 degrees- hand open) as shown in **Picture 304**. You are out of the line of fire momentarily. Remember, a check is not a re-directing motion. Don't push his knife arm or you will change the direction of his momentum and he will disconnect and re-attack. Not good. You want to dissolve him into you.

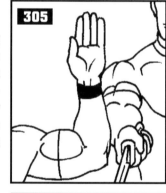

3. Slide your checking arm down and cup his arm as shown in **Picture 305** close-ups. Simultaneously punch him in the triangle as shown in picture **Picture 306**.

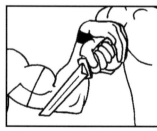

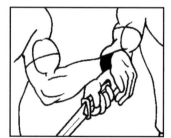

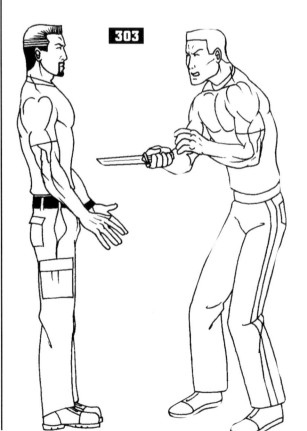

4. After the punch, you will either end up on the outside as shown (if the knife was in his right hand) or on the inside (if the knife was in his left hand).

5. Immediately after the punch, if you end up on the outside:

   a. Pass the knife to your left side as shown in **Picture 307**. This is accomplished by swinging his arm in front of you and scooping under it with your outside hand as shown in picture **Picture 308.** Do NOT step forward until the knife passes you. Then continue with step 6.

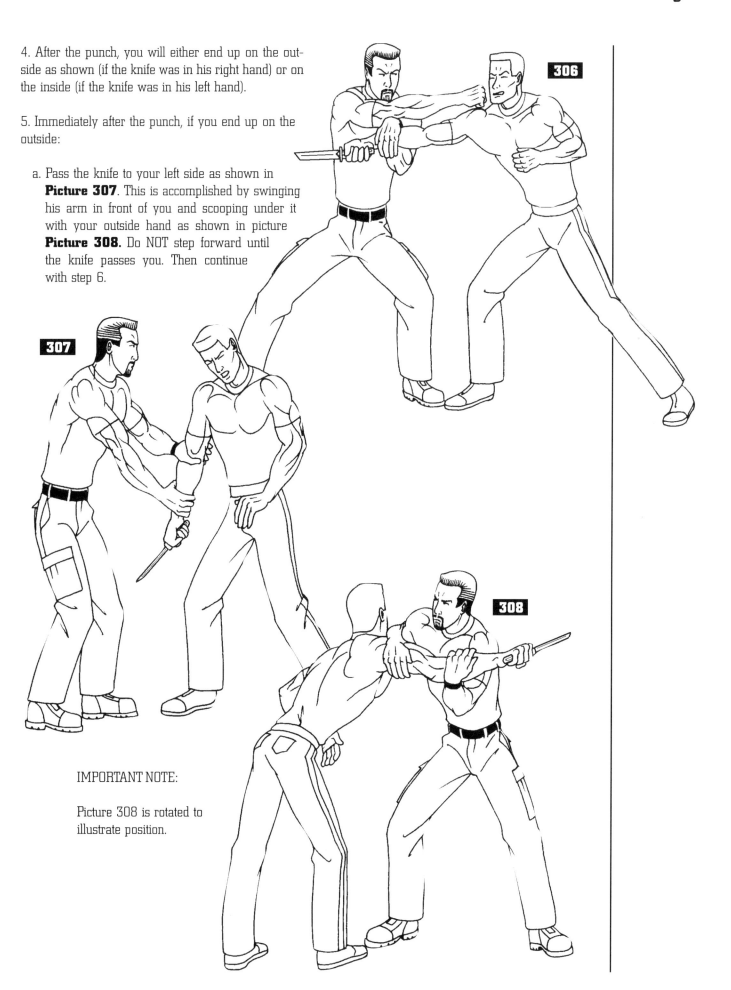

IMPORTANT NOTE:

Picture 308 is rotated to illustrate position.

Straight Stab

6. Immediately after the punch if you end up on the inside or immediately after step 4 if you were on the outside:

    a. Step in as shown in **Picture 309**, and

    b. Secure his knife arm to you as shown in **Picture 309**. You are hugging his arm to you tightly from underneath with your outside arm while gripping his armpit with your inside hand from over the top and pinning his shoulder to you. One up, one down- battery concept. Hold tightly and you are very secure.

    c. Make sure that your fore-arm is across his face as shown in **Picture 310** closeup. This will keep him from being able to switch the knife to his other hand. Without this, he can reach his other hand. It also makes any possible strike from his free hand far less effective.

    d. You are at your Point of Reference for most of the knife defenses.

    e. Deliver 3 knees as shown in **Picture 311, 312, and 313**. Do not disconnect. Stay tight.

f. Choose your objective:

Restrain and Disarm

(only recommended for law enforcement)

1. All disarms are done from a takedown
2. Push straight down on his neck (piston motion) to 6 o'clock as shown in **Picture 314 and 315**. Do not let go of his knife arm. He should be dropped right in front of you.
3. Drop down on his body with a knee and apply pressure to his neck with a knee as shown in picture **Picture 316**. Hit him if necessary.
4. Either strip the knife as shown in **Picture 317** or peel the knife out of his hand as shown in **Picture 318**. Peeling is the preferred method, and is done by squeezing his fingers closed by pressing on the finger nails to create pain and then digging your fingers under the knife handle and rolling his hand open

Incapacitate

1. Step on the forward foot as shown in **Picture 319**
2. Violently push away from you to break the ankle as shown in **Picture 320**. Push forward and toward the side holding the knife to avoid the knife whipping into you.

REFERENCE

Video Tape: **4**
◆ Section: **14.0**

DVD: **3**
Volume: **1**
Menu Chapter: **14**
◆ Section: **14.0**

Terminate

1. Slide your inside hand down his neck to his chin as shown in **Picture 321**. Stay tight. It can increase effectiveness to push his chin toward your body before wrenching.
2. Wrench violently up and back at an angle as shown in **Picture 322**.

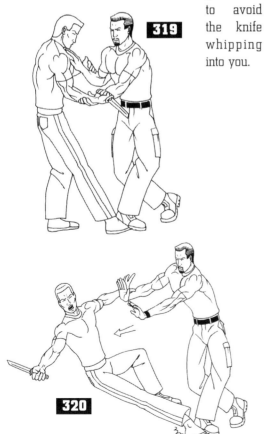

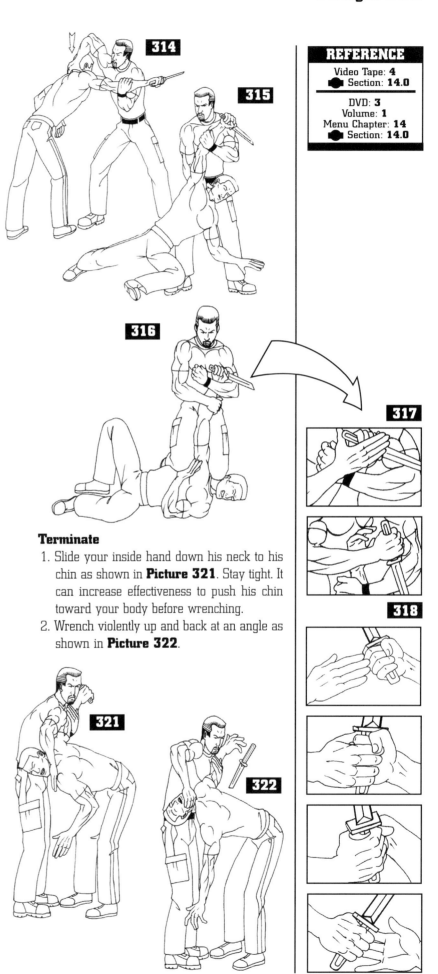

REFERENCE
Video Tape: **4**
■ Section: **13.0**

DVD: **3**
Volume: **1**
Menu Chapter: **13**
■ Section: **13.0**

F.I.G.H.T. Tip:
Containment
Do not use a strike which may repel your attacker and invite further attacks (such as a punch). The groin strike will help bring him in to you, so that you can contain him and end the engagement.

UNDERHAND STAB

Primary Danger – Knife Line of Travel

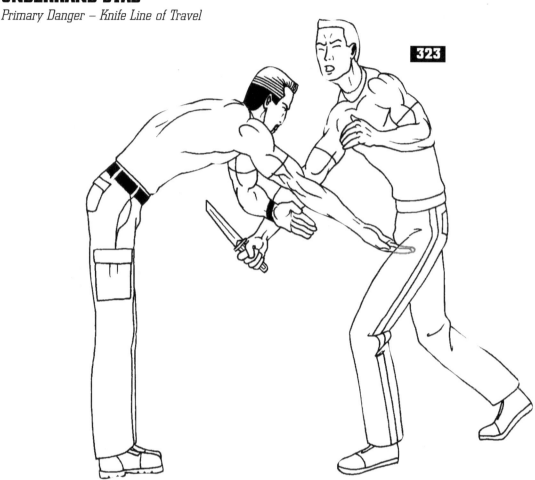

1. The attacker is swinging the knife at you from overhead as shown in **Picture 323**. This type of attack is not designed to scare you, it is designed to kill you and it is very difficult to defend against in reality, because it is usually used in a very tight encounter where the attacker is in very close and possibly holding you with his other hand where you may not see it coming. If you don't see it, it is too late.

2. Bend forward as shown in **Picture 323** and using your arm on the same side as he is stabbing from block the knife arm with your arm bent 90 degrees. It is important that you use a 90 degree block to have a secure block and that you bend forward to create sufficient space to ensure that the knife cannot reach you. It is also important that you use your same side arm to block. This is one of the few techniques that is not ambidextrous. That is you will have to program yourself to identify the hand the attacker is using and adjust your counter-attack accordingly.

3. Immediately hit his groin as shown in **Picture 323** with your other (inside) hand.

4. Swing the knife arm up and trap it from underneath with your blocking arm while using your other arm to grab by his armpit from over the top. Pull him in as shown in **Picture 324 and 325**. You have reached the same point of reference as in the angled knife attacks.

5. You are at your Point of Reference for most of the knife defenses.

6. Deliver 3 knees as shown in **Picture 326**, **327**, **and 328**. Do not disconnect. Stay tight.

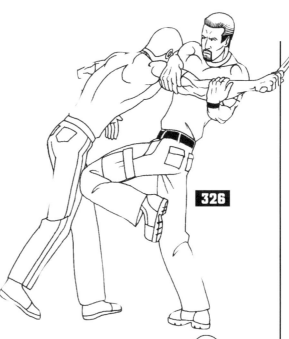

326

F.I.G.H.T. Note:
Images are rotated for illustration purposes.

324

F.I.G.H.T. Tip:
Point of Reference
Reminder- Keeping your forearm securely across the side of his face will keep him from switching hands with the knife and from effectively hitting you with his other hand. When you put your forearm across his face, do so violently- create damage with every touch.

325

327

328

Knife Threat Defenses

Underhand Stab

REFERENCE

Video Tape: **4**
Section: **14.0**

DVD: **3**
Volume: **1**
Menu Chapter: **14**
Section: **14.0**

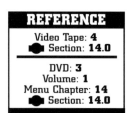

7. Choose your objective:

Restrain and Disarm

(only recommended for law enforcement)

a. All disarms are done from a takedown

b. Push straight down on his neck (piston motion) to 6 o'clock as shown in **Picture 329 and 330**. Do not let go of his knife arm. He should be dropped right in front of you.

c. Drop down on his body with a knee and apply pressure to his neck with a knee as shown in picture **Picture 331**. Hit him if necessary.

d. Either strip the knife as shown in **Picture 332** or peel the knife out of his hand as shown in **Picture 333**. Peeling is the preferred method, and is done by squeezing his fingers closed by pressing on the finger nails to create pain and then digging your fingers under the knife handle and rolling his hand open

Incapacitate

a. Step on the forward foot as shown in **Picture 334**

b. Violently push away from you to break the ankle as shown in **Picture 335**. Push forward and toward the side holding the knife to avoid the knife whipping into you.

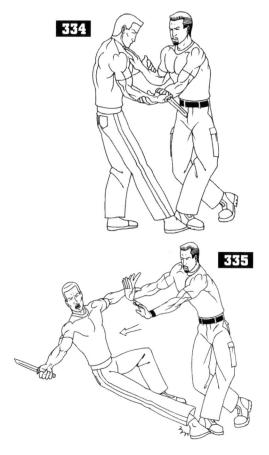

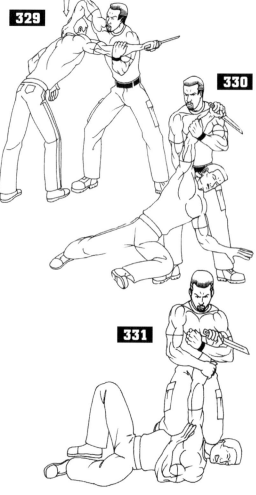

Terminate

a. Slide your inside hand down his neck to his chin as shown in **Picture 336**. Stay tight. It can increase effectiveness to push his chin toward your body before wrenching.

b. Wrench violently up and back at an angle as shown in **Picture 337**.

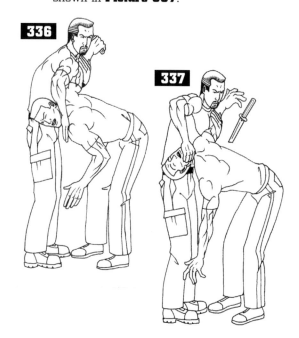

KNIFE THREAT TO THROAT FROM THE FRONT- KNIFE OUTSIDE

Primary Danger- The knife edge moving along your throat (this will then cut you)

1. The attacker is standing in front of you pressing the knife against your throat as shown in **Picture 338**. Typically, he will grab your shirt with the other hand as shown in **Picture 338**. You are not severely wounded unless he slides the knife along your throat. Therefore, you must keep this from occurring.

2. Comply. Begin your statement and raise your hands to about shoulder height (no higher) as shown in **Picture 338**. It is important when raising your hands not to go too high. It is also critical to note that one hand is inside his arms and one is outside. Therefore your hands are now placed one on each side of the arm holding the knife.

3. This action lowers his stress by making him think he will get what he wants and it brings your hands closer to the knife.

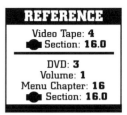

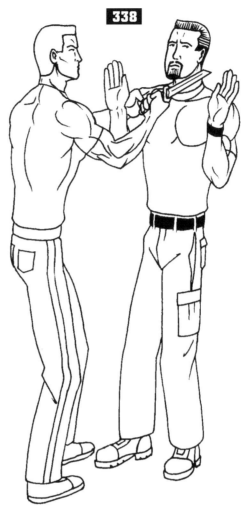

REFERENCE

Video Tape: **4**
◆ Section: **16.0**

DVD: **3**
Volume: **1**
Menu Chapter: **16**
◆ Section: **16.0**

F.I.G.H.T. Tip:
The hand on the outside when you raise your hands is the one on the same side as his knife arm his knife arm must be between your arms.

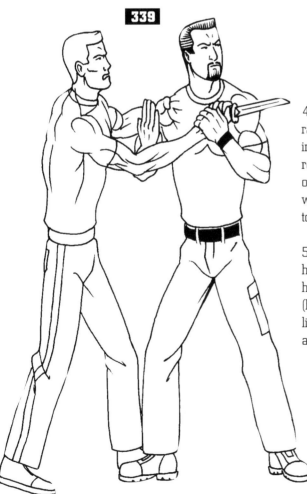

4. At about the middle of your compliance statement, rapidly strike the arm holding the knife while turning in the same direction as shown in **Picture 339**. The rotation moves the knife away from your throat without sliding it along your throat. It is important to hit when you turn mostly to block the knife's path back toward your throat.

5. Hitting the arm is also almost 'serving' the knife hand into your other hand. Immediately trap the knife hand **above the wrist** and pin it tightly to your chest (high) as shown in **Picture 339**. You are out of the line of fire. Note that the three actions- turning, hitting and pinning happen virtually simultaneously.

Knife Threat to Throat From The Front - Knife Outside

6. Smash your free hand into the "triangle" area behind and below his ear as shown in **Picture 340**.

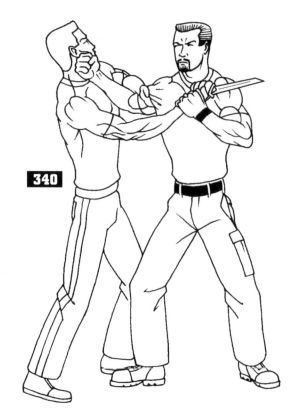

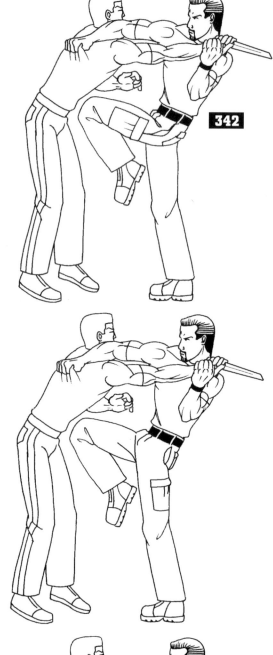

7. Slap your hand on his back and gather up his shirt as shown in **Picture 341**. You are now at a point of reference that is similar to POR 1 or 3 and to your knife point of reference.

8. Deliver 3 knees as shown in **Picture 342, 343, and 344**. Do not disconnect. Stay tight.

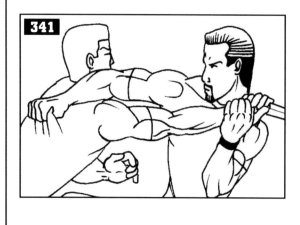

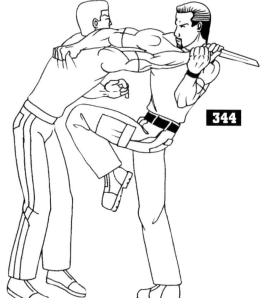

9. Choose your objective:

Restrain and Disarm

(only recommended for law enforcement)

a. All disarms are done from a takedown

b. Push straight down on his neck (piston motion) to 6 o'clock as shown in **Picture 345 and 346**. Do not let go of his knife arm. He should be dropped right in front of you.

c. Drop down on his body with a knee and apply pressure to his neck with a knee as shown in picture **Picture 347**. Hit him if necessary.

d. Either strip the knife as shown in **Picture 348** or peel the knife out of his hand as shown in **Picture 349**. Peeling is the preferred method, and is done by squeezing his fingers closed by pressing on the finger nails to create pain and then digging your fingers under the knife handle and rolling his hand open

Incapacitate

a. Step on the forward foot as shown in **Picture 350**

b. Violently push away from you to break the ankle as shown in **Picture 351**. Push forward and toward the side holding the knife to avoid the knife whipping into you.

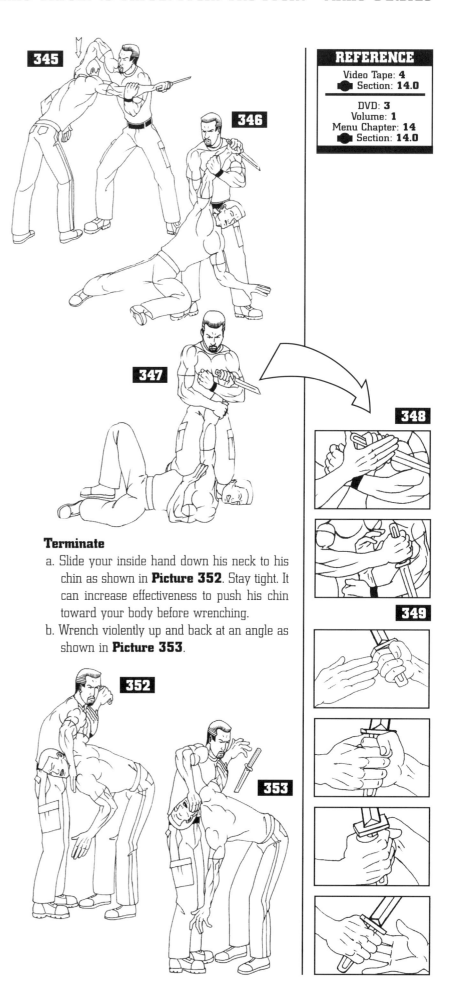

REFERENCE

Video Tape: **4**
Section: **14.0**

DVD: **3**
Volume: **1**
Menu Chapter: **14**
Section: **14.0**

Terminate

a. Slide your inside hand down his neck to his chin as shown in **Picture 352**. Stay tight. It can increase effectiveness to push his chin toward your body before wrenching.

b. Wrench violently up and back at an angle as shown in **Picture 353**.

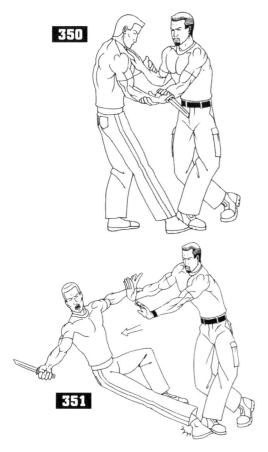

Knife Threat to Throat From The Front - Knife Inside

REFERENCE
Video Tape: **4**
◆ Section: **17.0**

DVD: **3**
Volume: **1**
Menu Chapter: **17**
◆ Section: **17.0**

KNIFE THREAT TO THROAT FROM THE FRONT- KNIFE INSIDE

Primary Danger- The knife edge moving along your throat (this will then cut you)

1. The attacker is standing in front of you pressing the knife against your throat as shown in **Picture 354**. Typically, he will grab your shirt with the other hand as shown in **Picture 354**. You are not severely wounded unless he slides the knife along your throat. Therefore, you must keep this from occurring.

2. Comply. Begin your statement and raise your hands to about shoulder height (no higher) as shown in **Picture 354**. It is important when raising your hands not to go too high. It is also critical to note that one hand is inside his arms and one is outside. Therefore your hands are now placed one on each side of the arm holding the knife.

3. This action lowers his stress by making him think he will get what he wants and it brings your hands closer to the knife.

F.I.G.H.T. Tip: Control
It is important to secure his hand to you fully. Secure by the hand, not by the wrist. This both keeps him from turning the blade in and prevents him from switching the knife into his other hand.

4. At about the middle of your compliance statement (after or as you say 'want'), with your outside hand, rapidly strike the arm holding the knife while turning your upper body in the same direction as shown in

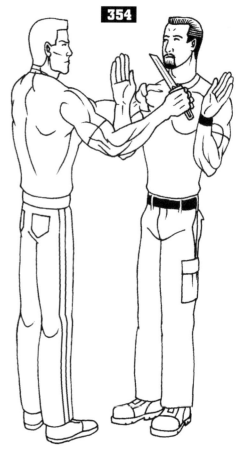

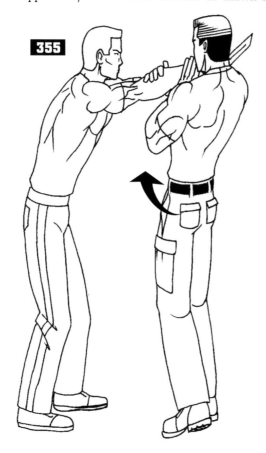

Picture 355. The rotation moves the knife away from your throat without sliding it along your throat. It is important to hit when you turn mostly to block the knife's path back toward your throat.

5. Hitting the arm is also almost 'serving' the knife hand into your other hand. Immediately trap the knife hand above the wrist and pin it tightly to your chest (high) as shown in **Picture 356** closeup. You are out of the line of fire. Note that the three actions - turning, hitting and pinning happen virtually simultaneously.

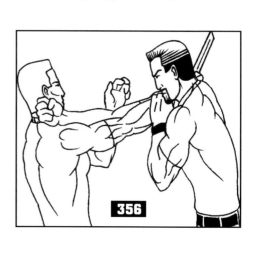

6. Smash your free hand into the "triangle" behind and below his ear as shown in **Picture 356**.

7. Slap your hand on his back and gather up his shirt as shown in picture **Picture 357**. You are now at appoint of reference that is similar to POR 1 or 3. However, this is a more vulnerable position because the knife remains accessible to his other hand. It is doubly important to move quickly from here.

Using the forearm across the attacker's face, push him away from you while maintaining a strong control. This should cause his free arm to disconnect.

8. Deliver 3 knees as shown in **Picture 357**, **358 and 359**. Do not disconnect. Stay tight.

Knife Threat to Throat From The Front - Knife Inside

REFERENCE
Video Tape: **4**
◆ Section: **14.0**

DVD: **3**
Volume: **1**
Menu Chapter: **14**
◆ Section: **14.0**

F.I.G.H.T. Tip:
*Do not attempt
to strip the knife
from the blade side.*

9. Choose your objective:

Restrain and Disarm

(only recommended for law enforcement)

a. All disarms are done from a takedown

b. Push straight down on his neck (piston motion) to 6 o'clock as shown in **Picture 360 and 361** Do not let go of his knife arm. He should be dropped right in front of you.

c. Drop down on his body with a knee and apply pressure to his neck with a knee as shown in picture **Picture 362**. Hit him if necessary.

d. Either strip the knife as shown in **Picture Series 363** or peel the knife out of his hand as shown in **Picture Series 364**. Peeling is the preferred method, and is done by squeezing his fingers closed by pressing on the finger nails to create pain and then digging your fingers under the knife handle and rolling his hand open

Incapacitate

a. Step on the forward foot as shown in **Picture 365**

b. Violently push away from you to break the ankle as shown in **Picture 366**. Push forward and toward the side holding the knife to avoid the knife whipping into you.

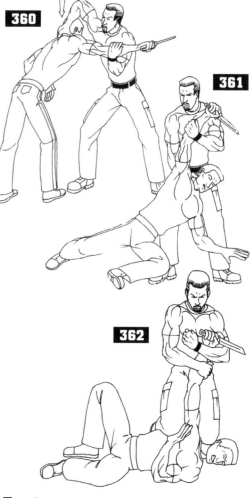

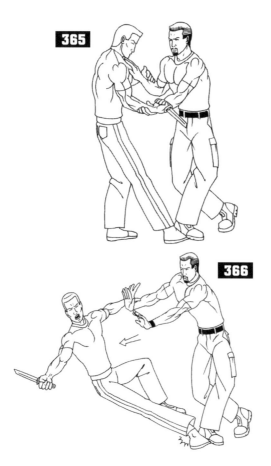

Terminate

a. Slide your inside hand down his neck to his chin as shown in **Picture 367**. Stay tight. It can increase effectiveness to push his chin toward your body before wrenching.

b. Wrench violently up and back at an angle as shown in **Picture 368**.

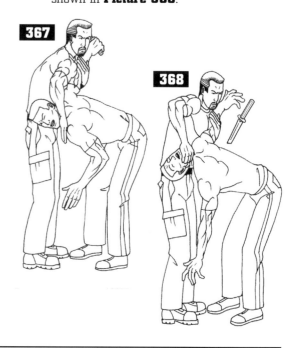

KNIFE THREAT TO THE THROAT FROM THE REAR- HOSTAGE STYLE

Primary Danger- The knife edge moving along your throat (this will then cut you)

1. The attacker is standing behind you pressing the knife against your throat as shown in **Picture 369**. He may also grab you with the other hand as shown in **Picture 369**. You are not severely wounded unless he slides the knife along your throat. Therefore, you must keep this from occurring.

2. Comply. Begin your statement and raise your hands to about shoulder height (no higher) as shown in **Picture 369**. It is important when raising your hands not to go too high.

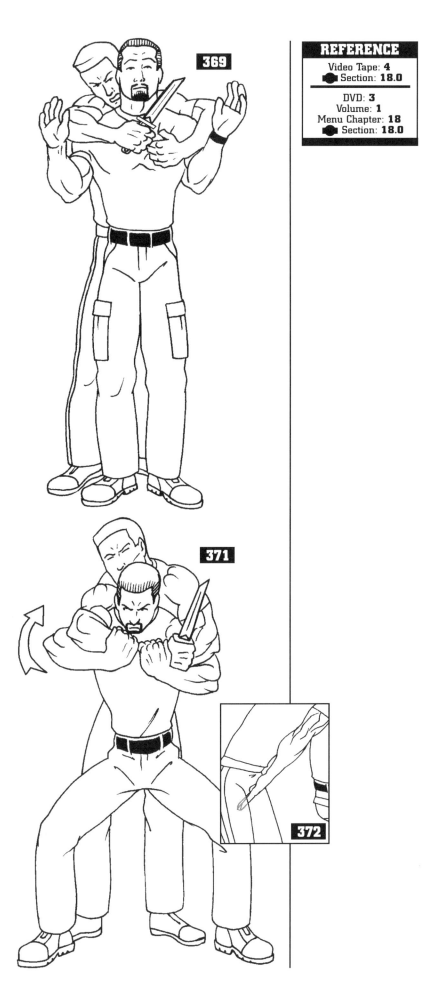

REFERENCE

Video Tape: **4**
◄ Section: **18.0**

DVD: **3**
Volume: **1**
Menu Chapter: **18**
◄ Section: **18.0**

3. This action lowers his stress by making him think he will get what he wants and it brings your hands closer to the knife.

4. At about the middle of your compliance statement (after or as you say 'want'), rapidly hook his hand holding the knife at the wrist and the hand itself using

Knife Threat to Throat From The Rear - Hostage Style

both of your hands as shown in **Picture 370**. As you hook, drop down slightly to base yourself as shown. It is important to hook the hand and wrist. Go too much toward the forearm and he may twist his wrist and still cut you with the knife. Too much toward the knife and you may grab the blade and cut yourself and let go.

5. Immediately release your grip with one hand (the hand on the same side from which the knife came from) and deliver a groin slap as shown in **Picture 372**.

6. Raise the shoulder his knife arm is over as shown in **Picture 371**. The raising of your shoulder creates an opening.

7. Step back through the opening with the leg opposite the shoulder you raised as shown in **Picture 373** and in the closeup view **Picture 374**.

8. Turn your body in and get behind him as shown in **Picture 375**.

9. Push his arm up as far as you can while bending him backwards as shown in **Picture 376**. Push with your hand that is on his wrist, bend with your other hand.

F.I.G.H.T. Tip:
Another Option
As shown in Picture 377, if necessary you can stab him while stepping behind him.

10. If he has not done so, tell him to drop the knife. If he does not react immediately, push violently upward and take the knife or stab with the knife if he remains violent and you fear for your life.

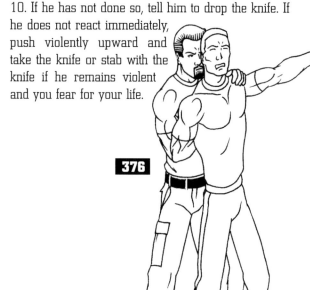

Gun Threat Defenses

One of the most stressful, violent encounters that could occur involves a person threatening you with a gun. You should assume that a person who would point a gun at you is perfectly willing to kill you. Most people's only experience with guns is either in a controlled setting such as target shooting or other sport shooting, or their only knowledge of guns is from TV and what they see on the news. For those of you with no experience with guns we strongly recommend that you take a course at a local range to get a basic familiarity with how they function. You don't have to decide to own a gun. But you should know how one of the most dangerous weapons a criminal might confront you with works. Why? Let's briefly look to the movies. You see a scene where a criminal armed with a gun confronts an everyday person. Somehow (typically unrealistically) they manage to hit the guy and have a chance to get away. Many times they leave the gun and run. Sometimes they pick up the gun and throw it away, then run. Neither is a very good idea as the criminal, who knows how to use the gun, can pick up the gun. Now you have a really angry criminal who now knows you aren't cooperating and has a gun. Very bad. Sometimes, the person picks up the gun and points it at the criminal but it's obvious they don't know what they are doing (safety is on, etc). Very bad. And sometimes, although the character supposedly is not familiar with how the gun works, they shoot the criminal. Despite what you read about accidental shootings, deliberately shooting a person with a gun you just took from them is unlikely if you are unfamiliar with guns for too many reasons to go into. So, if you are serious about being able to handle a situation where you are confronted by a gun wielding assailant, studying these techniques will enable you to get his gun in your hands, but you need to learn how to use it. For those of you that do have some experience with guns (and even for those of you that don't, but want to learn self defense as opposed to target oriented shooting), IDFS offers Combat Shooting as part of its series. Additional combat shooting training is also beneficial for military and law enforcement. Go to *www.fight2survive.com* for information.

There are some basics that are true of virtually all guns and that are the basis for the techniques that are included here.

- Guns discharge (fire a bullet) when the trigger is pulled (safety off, bullet in chamber)

- It takes very little pressure to pull the trigger

- Guns shoot the bullet essentially in a straight line extending out to wherever the gun is pointing when the trigger is pulled (the 'Line of Fire')

- Guns are very loud. If a gun discharges near you, you will be startled and your ears will be ringing. Even if you expect it.

- If you interfere with the normal operation of certain parts of a gun during the firing process, it will probably become jammed, rendering it incapable of firing again until the problem is fixed. On a

semi-automatic weapon, this would be the slide that moves backward and then forward violently when discharged. See **Picture 378**. On a revolver, this would be the cylinder, which spins when dis-

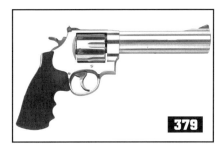

charged. See **Picture 379**.

In general, we operate on the assumption that if a person threatens you with a gun, it is better to take away the gun, if possible, than to leave your life in his hands. If the threat is one that you learn to defend against in this program, you gain the chance to disarm your attacker. If not, cooperate until you are in one of these scenarios or can move into one. If that is not safely possible or you do not feel confident then you will have to simply cooperate.

When discussing gun threats, we mean that a person that is pointing a gun at you and is making, or will make, a demand. Generally, if a person with a gun wants you dead as a <u>primary</u> objective, he will shoot you from a distance. If your attacker maintains his distance, these techniques become irrelevant. If he pushes a gun into you, or comes very close and does not shoot you, he likely has a demand. The fact that he has a demand keeps you alive and gives you time to react.

Demands are typically in three categories: possessions

F.I.G.H.T. Tip:
How to get closer to an attacker with a gun is covered in the Advanced Tactics Series, Volume II. Also, how to execute gun disarms when more than one bystander is present is covered in that series.

Summary

(give me your money, etc.), your body (rape, abduction, etc), or information (where is something, did you do something, etc.). In each case, the psychology of the situation is that when the assailant jams his gun into or points his gun at you and makes a demand, he feels powerful, in control sure he will get what he wants. He is also probably nervous. He does not want this to take long, and he does not want to get caught. That is why virtually every gun threat covered in the F.I.G.H.T. series starts with you raising your hands to a certain level, depending upon the situation (between slightly off your sides to shoulder height – no higher), and beginning a statement similar to "I'll do whatever you want. What do you want?" By stating that you will do whatever your attacker wants, you help take the edge off him and play off his psychological momentum by making him think his assault is going to work. Just as important, your starting line will help you compose yourself and focus on the disarm techniques that follow. This initial response is the first element in every gun threat and we call it 'complying'. Remember, you do not have to complete the statement. You can act near the end. In fact, it may be better to act while you are talking but it is important that you are talking when you act.

The second element in each technique is eliminating the primary danger. Many people think that the primary danger in a gun threat is the gun itself or getting shot, or the attacker pulling the trigger. In reality, the primary danger is that you are in the "line of fire", the place where the bullet will go if the gun is discharged. If you are able to get out of the line of fire before the trigger is pulled, you are momentarily out of danger from the gun. At this point you are endangered by your attacker's ability to get you back into the line of fire. The following techniques take away his ability to do so.

You should now review the first gun threat to familiarize yourself with the techniques involved, and then examine the psychological responses of your attacker explained herein that make these techniques so effective.

PSYCHOLOGY OF DISARMS

By examining the psychology of the gun threat defenses using this first one, you see why they are so devastating and effective. At the outset, the attacker feels powerful and possibly nervous or completely dominant. He is ready to get what he wants. You comply. He feels even better. As his state of mind improves, suddenly you get control of the gun. It goes off. Bang! You are still there. A stunning reversal begins to occur. Before he even has a chance to process what just happened, he feels a sharp pain in his chest from the impact of the barrel and an excruciating pain in his hand from his finger breaking. He looks down and all of the skin and meat has been ripped from his finger. He is shocked. He hears you yelling 'Get on the floor!' He looks up and sees his gun in your hands pointing at him. Surprise! Pain! Damage! More pain! Noise! Shock! These are the things that, if they come one right after the other, keep your attacker from reacting effectively and result with you in control of the gun. They are common to all of these gun disarms. More importantly, each technique starts by getting you out of the line of fire and then keeps you there throughout.

Our techniques are designed to assume:

- The gun will discharge while you are attempting to get it, but will be jammed once you have taken it.
- The attacker will resist you taking the gun. His first reaction will be to yank back.
- There may be bystanders you are trying to protect if possible

Learn these techniques well and you will be able to maintain your composure in the most stressful situation. The person who is most composed and focused is in control, regardless of who has the gun. Practice.

GUN THREAT FRONT- HIGH (HEAD)

Primary danger-Line of Fire (get out of it)

1. The attacker is standing in front of you holding a gun pointed at your head similar to **Picture 380**. The gun can be touching your head or not, but it must be within reach of your hands for this to be effective.

2. Comply. Begin your statement and raise your hands to shoulder height as shown in **Picture 380**. It is important when raising your hands not to go too high, and to keep them close to your body.

3. This action lowers your attacker's stress by making him think he will get what he wants and it brings your hands closer to the gun.

4. At about the middle of your compliance statement (after or as you say 'want'), rapidly **drop down** by widening your feet in a quick move and simultaneously shoot your hands up under the gun grabbing it near the trigger guard as shown in **Picture 381**. You are out of the line of fire. Note the following important points:

    a. Your hands are 'pigeoned' together as shown in **Picture 382**

    b. You are securing the gun at the trigger guard. Avoid grabbing just the barrel because it is too

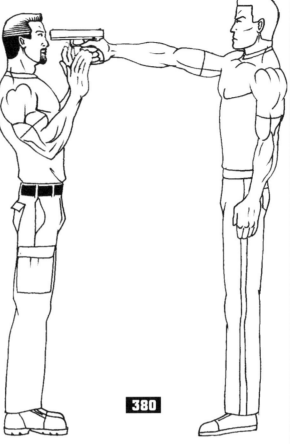

380

easy for him to rip the gun out of your hands and if the barrel is 'compensated' (has holes in the top), you may burn your hands when the gun discharges, and you will not jam a revolver.

REFERENCE

Video Tape: **5**
◆ Section: **5.0**

DVD: **3**
Volume: **2**
Menu Chapter: **5**
◆ Section: **5.0**

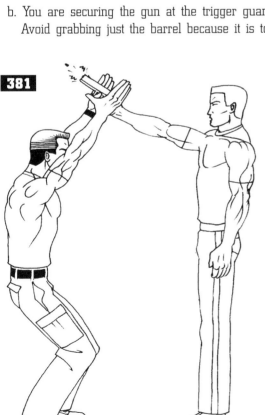

381

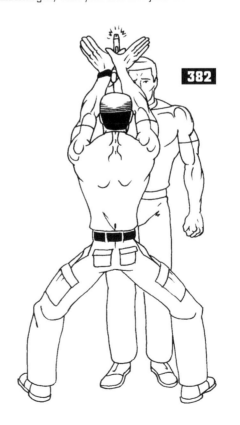

382

Gun Threat Front - High (Head)

5. When you touch the gun, he will likely involuntarily shoot (discharge) it once. Do not worry; you are out of the line of fire. Loud bang. Ears ringing. He is surprised because you caused the discharge and he didn't expect it. The gun is likely jammed because your hands also grabbed the slide (or cylinder, if a revolver) and interfered with its operation when you secured the gun by the trigger guard.

6. Immediately, tightly rotate the gun up and over to point it at him as shown in **Picture 383**; you may break his finger.

7. Step in strongly with your strong side leg and **slam** the barrel of the gun into him, preferably at chest height as shown in **Picture 384**. He may have already let go of the gun. Keep going.

8. Swing your strong side leg back out while ripping the gun straight backwards with you out of his hand(s) as shown in **Picture 385** (reverse image). You will probably break his finger and may pull the skin off the bone in the process of this disarm. Either way, he is stunned and in pain.

9. Create distance between you and the attacker by taking three steps back, then rack the slide to clear the jam, and as shown in **Picture 386** with closeups, point the gun at him and tell him to get on the floor. **Picture 387** It would be a good idea to glance at the gun and be sure the safety (if any) is off.

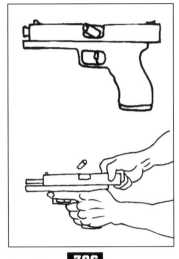

386

10. If he resumes his attack and you are in fear for your life (and a reasonable person would testify as such), in most jurisdictions you are justified to shoot. Otherwise while he remains on the ground call the police or have someone do so. When they arrive and likely draw their guns- do exactly as they say. They don't know who the bad guy is. Do not under any circumstances point the gun in the direction of the police.

387

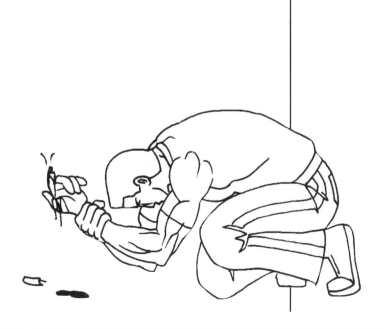

Gun Threat Front - Low - Pointing at the Neck or Below (Typically the Chest)

**F.I.G.H.T. Tip:
Alternative
Technique**

*This disarm can also be
used with the gun point-
ed at your head instead
of the previous disarm
to the head if the gun is
out of reach for that disarm. However, the risk
of bystander fatality is
increased by doing so
due to the height of the
re-directed line of fire at
time of discharge if the
gun is to your head*

GUN THREAT FRONT- LOW –
POINTING AT THE NECK OR BELOW
(TYPICALLY THE CHEST)

Primary danger-Line of Fire (get out of it)

1. The attacker is standing in front of you holding a gun
pointed at your chest (as high as your neck or as low
as your abdomen) similar to **Picture 388**. The gun
can be touching you or not, but it must be within reach
of your hands for this to be effective.

2. Comply. Begin your statement and raise your hands
to about the same height as the gun, no higher as
shown in **Picture 388**. It is important when raising
your hands not to go too high, and to keep them close
to your body.

3. This action lowers his stress by making him think he
will get what he wants and it brings your hands closer to the gun

4. At about the middle of your compliance statement
(after or as you say 'want'), rapidly turn your upper
body to your strong side and shoot out your front
(weaker) hand grabbing the gun around the trigger
guard as shown in **Picture 389**. This turning action
removes you from the line of fire.

5. When you touch the gun, he will likely involuntarily
shoot (discharge) it once. Don't worry; you are out of

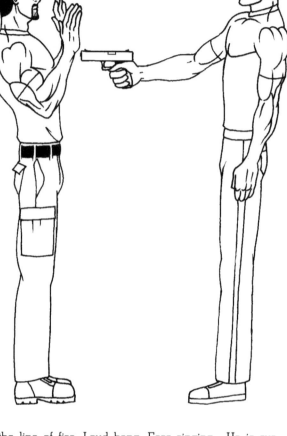

the line of fire. Loud bang. Ears ringing. He is surprised because you caused the discharge and he didn't
expect it. The gun is likely jammed because your hands
grabbing around it at the trigger guard also grabbed

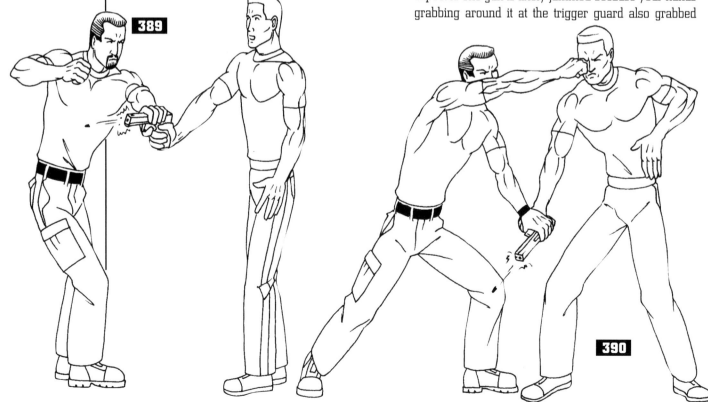

Gun Threat Front - Low - Pointing at the Neck or Below (Typically the Chest)

the slide (or cylinder, if a revolver) and interfered with its operation.

6. While pushing the gun down and away, step in with

your weak side foot and deliver a cross with your rear hand to his neck or face. Aim behind and below the ear as shown in **Picture 390**, but hit whatever is available.

7. Slide your free hand down under the gun in **Picture 391** (do not cross in front of the gun) and grab the back corner of the gun near the hammer as shown in **Picture 392 and 393**.

8. Rip the gun out by rotating it around and on a diagonal as shown in **Picture 394**, while swinging your leg backwards for increased leverage.

9. Depending upon which hand he had holding the gun you may break his finger and rip off the skin.

10. Create distance between you and the attacker by taking three steps back, and then rack the slide to clear the jam, and as shown in **Picture 395**, point the gun at him and tell him to get on the floor. It would be a good idea to glance at the gun and be sure the safety (if any) is off.

11. If he resumes his attack and you are in fear for your life (and a reasonable person would testify as such), in most jurisdictions you are justified to shoot. Otherwise while he remains on the ground call the police or have someone do so. When they arrive and likely draw their guns- do exactly as they say. They don't know who the bad guy is. Do not under any circumstances point the gun in the direction of the police.

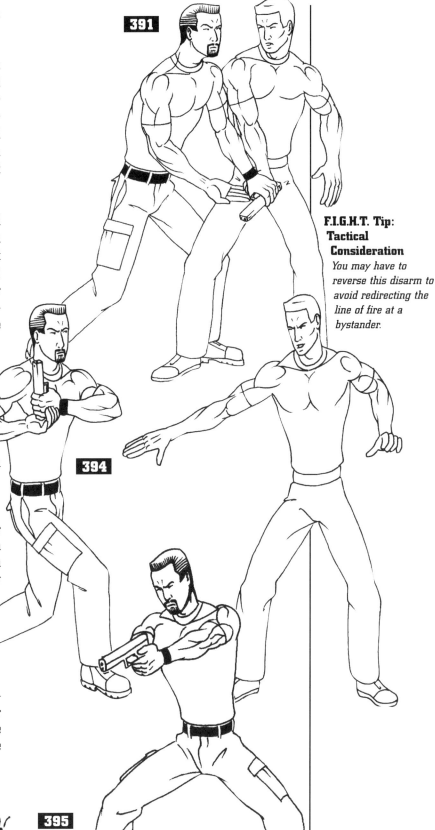

F.I.G.H.T. Tip:
Tactical
Consideration
You may have to reverse this disarm to avoid redirecting the line of fire at a bystander.

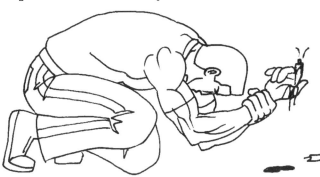

Gun Threat Defenses

Gun Threat Front - Low - Pointing Up Under The Chin

REFERENCE

Video Tape: **5**
Section: **6.0**

DVD: **3**
Volume: **2**
Menu Chapter: **6**
Section: **6.0**

F.I.G.H.T. Tip:
Raising your hands is natural when confronted. However, do no move abruptly. Composure and faking fear and compliance is essential.

GUN THREAT FRONT- LOW – POINTING UP UNDER THE CHIN
Primary danger-Line of Fire (get out of it)

1. The attacker is standing in front of you pressing the gun upward under your chin. He may grab your shirt with the other hand as shown in **Picture 396**. The key difference here is that you will not be able to get out of the line of fire by moving your head, because the gun will follow. Therefore, you must move the gun.

2. Comply. Begin your statement and raise your hands to about shoulder height (no higher) as shown in picture **Picture 396** do not duplicate. It is important when raising your hands not to go too high. It is also critical to note that one hand is inside his arms and one is outside. Therefore your hands are now placed one on each side of the arm holding the gun.

3. This action lowers his stress by making him think he will get what he wants and it brings your hands closer to the gun.

4. At about the middle of your compliance statement (after or as you say 'want'), rapidly turn your upper body toward the gun hand and strike the arm holding

the gun in the same direction, as shown in **Picture 397**.

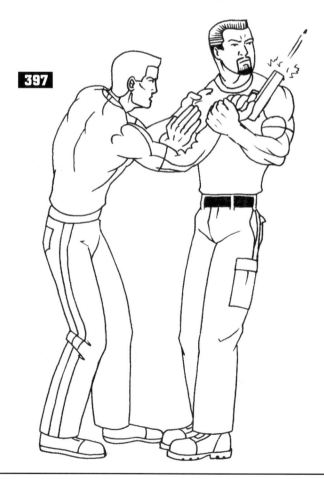

5. Hitting the arm is almost 'serving' the gun into your other hand. Immediately trap the gun hand above the wrist and pin it tightly to your chest (high) as shown in **Picture 397**. You are out of the line of fire.

6. When you touch the gun, he will likely involuntarily shoot (discharge) it. **Picture 398.** Don't worry; you are out of the line of fire. Loud bang. Ears ringing. He is surprised because you caused the discharge and he didn't expect it. The gun is probably **not** jammed because your hands did not interfere with the slide (or cylinder, if a revolver). He may continue discharging it. Work smoothly.

7. Smash your free hand into the area behind and below his ear as shown in **Picture 399**.

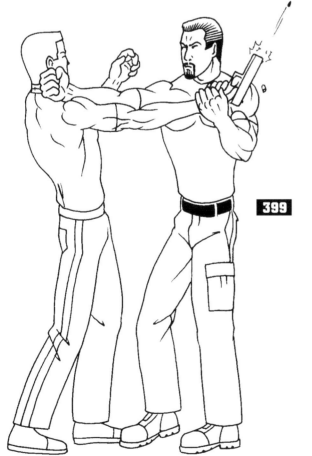

8. Slap your hand on his back and gather up his shirt as shown in **Picture 400**. Knee him forcefully and step forward to disrupt his balance. Keep a tight grip on the gun.

F.I.G.H.T. Tip: Securing Gun
It is essential that the gun be secured by the hand, not the wrist. If you pin it to you by the wrist, the attacker can still rotate the gun and direct the line of fire back at you.

Gun Threat Front - Low - Pointing Up Under The Chin

9. Reach over the gun with your free hand as shown in **Picture 401** and grab the slide/top as shown in **Picture 402**. Note the turned position of your hand with the thumb on the outside side of the gun. This position will give you the leverage necessary to break the gun free.

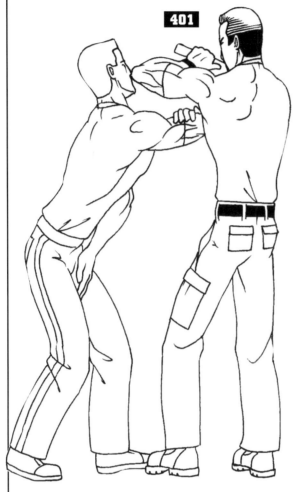

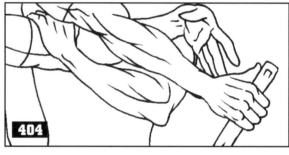

11. Deliver an elbow to the face as shown in **Picture 405**.

12. Take three steps back, rack the slide to clear any possible jam, point the gun at him and tell him to get on the floor. It would be a good idea to glance at the gun and be sure the safety (if any) is off.

13. If he resumes his attack and you are in fear for your life (and a reasonable person would see the situation as you do), in most jurisdictions you are justified to shoot. Otherwise while he remains on the floor call the police or have someone do so. When they arrive and likely draw their guns - do exactly as they say. They don't know who the bad guy really is. Do not under any circumstances point the gun in the direction of the police.

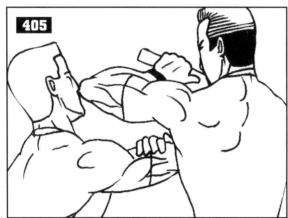

10. Twist your hand sharply 90 degrees and 'punch out' straight with the gun to take it away as shown in **Picture 402, 403, and 404**.

GUN THREAT SIDE - HEAD OR NECK IN FRONT OF THE EAR

Primary danger-Line of Fire (get out of it)

1. The attacker is standing beside you holding a gun pointed at your head (or neck) in front of your ear similar to **Picture 406**.

2. Comply. Begin your statement and raise your hands to shoulder height, no higher, as shown in **Picture 407**. It is important when raising your hands not to go too high, and to keep them close to your body.

3. This action lowers his stress by making him think he will get what he wants and it brings your hands closer to the gun

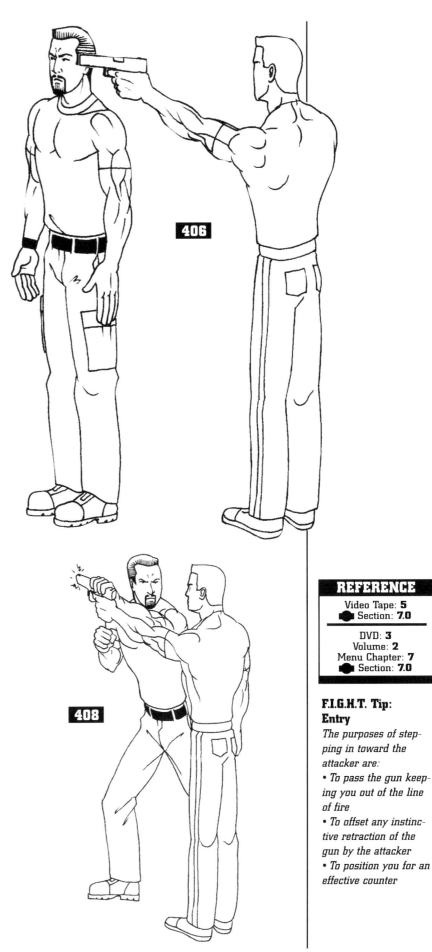

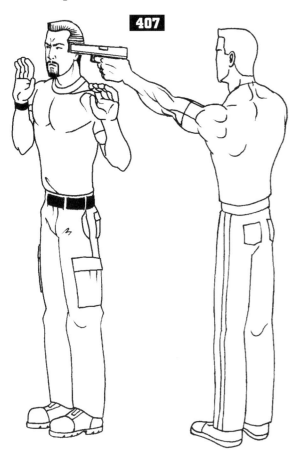

4. At about the middle of your compliance statement (after or as you say 'want'), rapidly lean back and step back at an angle **toward** the attacker with the foot closest to him as in **Picture 408**. Simultaneously grab the gun at the trigger guard with your hand closest to the gun as shown.

5. When you touch the gun, he will likely involuntarily shoot (discharge) it. Don't worry; you are out of the line

REFERENCE

Video Tape: **5**
◆ Section: **7.0**

DVD: **3**
Volume: **2**
Menu Chapter: **7**
◆ Section: **7.0**

F.I.G.H.T. Tip:
Entry
The purposes of stepping in toward the attacker are:
• *To pass the gun keeping you out of the line of fire*
• *To offset any instinctive retraction of the gun by the attacker*
• *To position you for an effective counter*

Gun Threat Side - High - Head Or Neck In Front Of The Ear

of fire. Loud bang. Ears ringing. He is surprised because you caused the discharge and he didn't expect it. The gun is now jammed because your hands grabbing around it at the trigger guard also grabbed the slide (or cylinder if a revolver) and interfered with its operation.

6. While pushing the gun down and away, pivot toward him and punch him in the face with your free hand as in **Pictures 409 and 410**.

7. Slide the hand you just punched with down under the gun (do not cross in front of the gun) and grab the back corner of the gun near the hammer as shown in **Picture 411 and 412**.

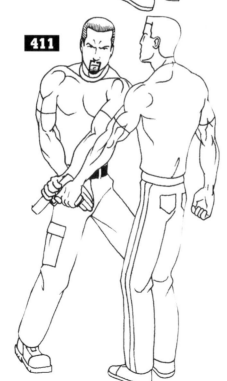

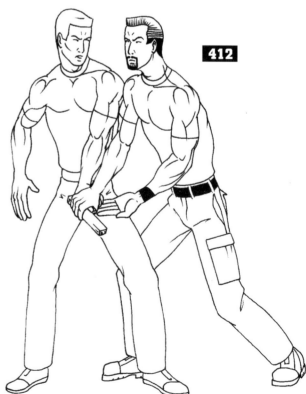

Gun Threat Side - High - Head Or Neck In Front Of The Ear

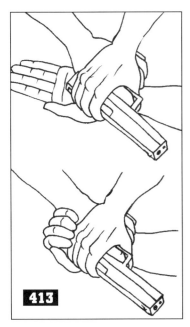

413

8. Rip the gun out by rotating it around and on a diagonal as shown in **Picture 413** while swinging the leg closest to your attacker backwards for increased leverage as shown in **Picture 414**.

9. Take three steps back, rack the slide to clear the jam, and as shown in **Picture 415**, point the gun at him and tell him to get on the floor. It would be a good idea to glance at the gun and be sure the safety (if any) is off.

10. If he resumes his attack and you are in fear for your life (and a reasonable person would see the situation as you do), in most jurisdictions you are justified to shoot. Otherwise while he remains on the floor call the police. When they arrive and likely draw their guns- do exactly as they say. They don't know who the bad guy really is. Do not under any circumstances point the gun in the direction of the police.

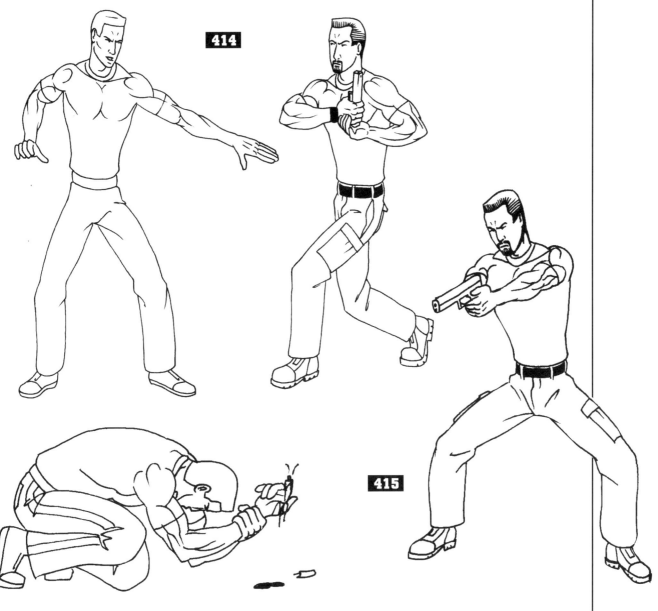

414

415

Gun Threat Side - High - Head Behind The Ear

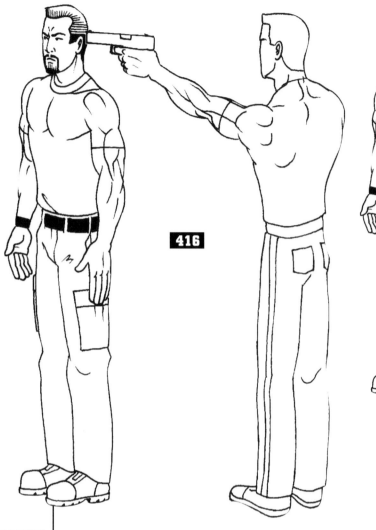

416

417

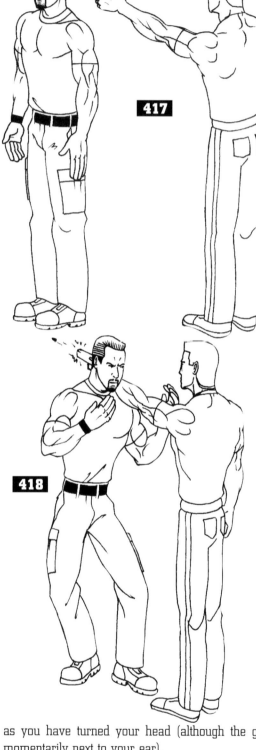

418

REFERENCE

Video Tape: **5**
Section: **8.0**

DVD: **3**
Volume: **2**
Menu Chapter: **8**
Section: **8.0**

GUN THREAT SIDE- HIGH- HEAD BEHIND THE EAR

Primary danger-Line of Fire (get out of it)

1. The attacker is standing beside you holding a gun pointed at your head (or neck) behind your ear similar to **Picture 416**.

2. Comply. Begin your statement and raise your hands to shoulder height, no higher. It is important when raising your hands not to go too high, and to keep them close to your body.

3. This action lowers his stress by making him think he will get what he wants and it brings your hands closer to the gun

4. At about the middle of your compliance statement (after or as you say 'want'), rapidly turn your head and upper body toward the attacker and **step in with the leg closest to him (passing the gun)** while trapping his gun arm by wrapping your arm under it as shown in **Picture 418**. You are out of the line of fire as soon

as you have turned your head (although the gun is momentarily next to your ear).

5. When you touch the gun, he will likely involuntarily shoot (discharge) it once. Don't worry; you are out of the line of fire. Loud bang. Ears ringing. He is surprised because you caused the discharge and he didn't expect it. The sound will hurt. Your adrenaline will help you.

The gun is now probably not jammed because your hands did not necessarily touch the slide (or cylinder if a revolver) and interfere with its operation. He may keep discharging the gun. (Do not panic -) Keep working.

6. As you step in and trap his arm as described in step #4, hit him with your free arm elbow as shown in **Picture 419**.

7. With your rear leg, knee him as shown in **Picture 420** and **step forcefully through him** to disrupt his balance. Do not pull your leg back upon striking with the knee, simply step forward pushing him back. Keep a strong grip with your trapping arm. Do not let the gun arm get loose.

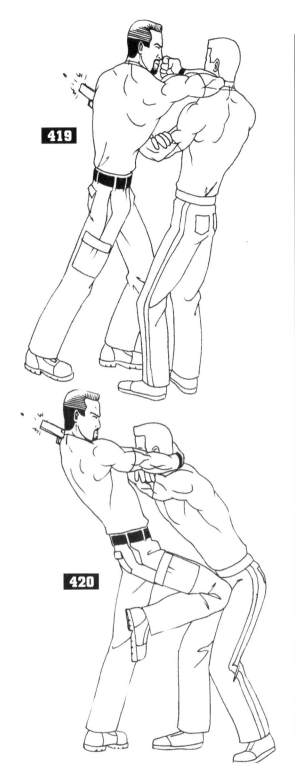

419

420

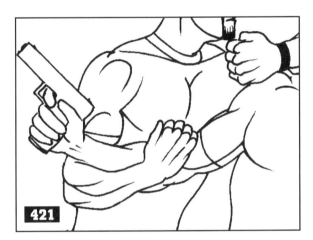

421

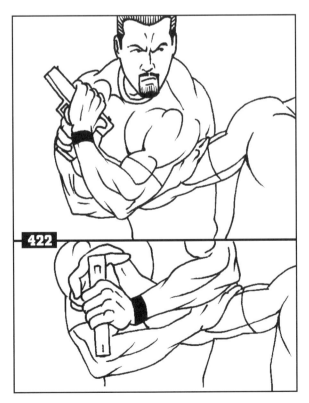

422

F.I.G.H.T. Tip: Trapping
When trapping the gun arm, your hand should end up on his upper arm above his elbow.

BALANCE
When you step through after kneeing to disrupt his balance, you can push him with your free arm. However, don't push him so hard that your grip on the gun is fighting your own strength.

8. Reach over the gun with your free hand, as shown in **Pictures 421 and 422**, and grab the slide/top as shown. Note the turned position of your hand with the thumb on the outside side of the gun. This position will give you the leverage necessary to break the gun free.

Gun Threat Side - High - Head Behind The Ear

9. Twist your hand sharply 90 degrees and 'punch out' straight with the gun to take it away as shown in **Picture 423**.

F.I.G.H.T. Tip:
Finger Breaks
Finger breaks may not occur. It depends upon a number of factors.

10. Deliver an elbow to the face as shown in **Picture 424**.

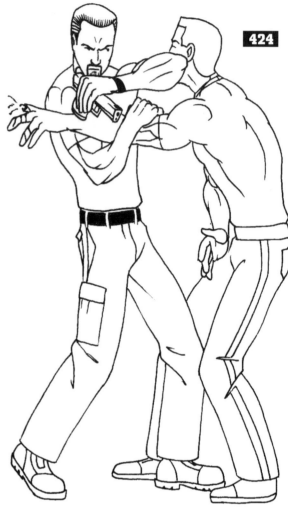

11. Take three steps back, rack the slide to clear the jam, and as shown in **Picture 425**, point the gun at him and tell him to get on the floor. It would be a good idea to glance at the gun and be sure the safety (if any) is off.

12. If he resumes his attack and you are in fear for your life (and a reasonable person would see the situation as you do), in most jurisdictions you are justified to shoot. Otherwise while he remains on the floor call the police or have someone else do so. When they arrive and likely draw their guns- do exactly as they say. They don't know who the bad guy really is. Do not under any circumstances point the gun in the direction of the police.

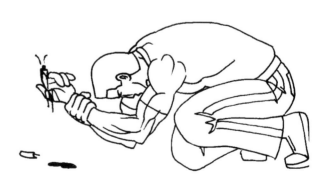

GUN THREAT SIDE- SIDE OF BODY, IN FRONT OF THE ARM

Primary danger-Line of Fire (get out of it)

1. The attacker is standing beside you holding a gun pointed at your side in front of your arm similar to **Picture 426**.

2. Comply. Begin your statement and open your hands neutrally as shown in **Picture 427**. This action lowers his stress by making him think he will get what he wants, but it doesn't bring your hands closer to the gun. In this position, moving your hands much closer to the gun would seem unnatural and may provoke a response. Simply open them.

REFERENCE

Video Tape: **5**
Section: **9.0**

DVD: **3**
Volume: **2**
Menu Chapter: **9**
Section: **9.0**

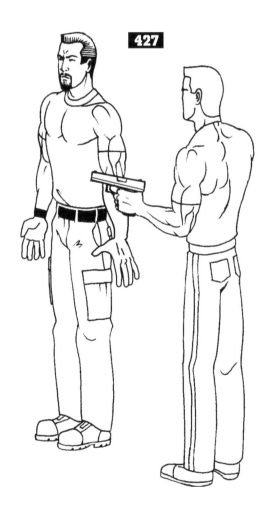

3. At about the middle of your compliance statement (after or as you say 'want'), rapidly 'scoop' your body back as shown in **Picture 428**. This is accomplished by almost hopping backward while allowing your upper body to slightly collapse forward. You are out of the line of fire.

Gun Threat Side - Low - Side of Body - In Front Of The Arm

4. Simultaneously, grab the gun at the trigger guard with your hand furthest from the gun and the attacker's wrist with your hand closest to him as shown in **Picture 429**. Keep your elbows tight to your body.

5. When you touch the gun, he will likely involuntarily shoot (discharge) it. Don't worry; you are out of the line of fire. Loud bang. Ears ringing. He is surprised because you caused the discharge and he didn't expect it. . The gun is now jammed because your hand grabbing around it at the trigger guard also grabbed the slide (or cylinder, if a revolver) and interfered with its operation.

6. Tightly turn your body toward the attacker while simultaneously turning the gun 180 degrees as shown in **Picture 430**. Note that the gun is pointing toward the attacker.

7. Step in with your inside foot (the one in front of his body) and ram the gun barrel into his upper body hard.

8. Step strongly back with your inside foot, simultaneously ripping the gun out of his hand(s) as shown in **Picture 431**.

9. Take three steps back, rack the slide to clear the jam, and as shown in **Picture 432**, point the gun at him and tell him to get on the floor. It would be a good idea to glance at the gun and be sure the safety (if any) is off.

10. If he resumes his attack and you are in fear for your life (and a reasonable person would see the situation as you do), in most jurisdictions you are justified to shoot. Otherwise while he remains on the floor call the police or have someone else do so. When they arrive and likely draw their guns - do exactly as they say. They don't know who the bad guy really is. Do not under any circumstances point the gun in the direction of the police.

Gun Threat Side - Low - Side of Body - In Front Of The Arm

431

432

F.I.G.H.T. Tip:
Positioning
His grip on the gun (one hand, two hands) and the hand he uses to hold the gun (left, right) will not affect the steps taken to disarm. It may cause you to be on his inside or outside. You have no control over that. In disarms with gun rotation, this may affect whether his finger is broken. In disarms with kneeing it will affect the target for the knee strike.

Gun Threat Side - Low - Side of Body - Behind The Arm

REFERENCE

Video Tape: **5**
◆ Section: **10.0**

DVD: **3**
Volume: **2**
Menu Chapter: **10**
◆ Section: **10.0**

GUN THREAT SIDE- SIDE OF BODY, BEHIND THE ARM

Primary danger-Line of Fire (get out of it)

1. The attacker is standing behind you holding a gun pointed at the side of your body with the gun behind your arm. (back shown) similar to **Picture 433**

2. Comply. Begin your statement and open your hands neutrally as shown in **Picture 433**. This action lowers his stress by making him think he will get what he wants, but it doesn't bring your hands closer to the gun. In this position moving your hands much closer to the gun would seem unnatural and may provoke a response. Simply open them.

3. At about the middle of your compliance statement (after or as you say 'want'), rapidly turn toward the attacker and step in with the leg closest to him (passing the gun) while trapping his gun arm by wrapping your arm under it as shown in pictures **Picture 434 and 435**. You are out of the line of fire as soon as you have turned your body.

F.I.G.H.T. Tip: Trapping
When trapping the gun arm, your hand should end up on his upper arm above his elbow.

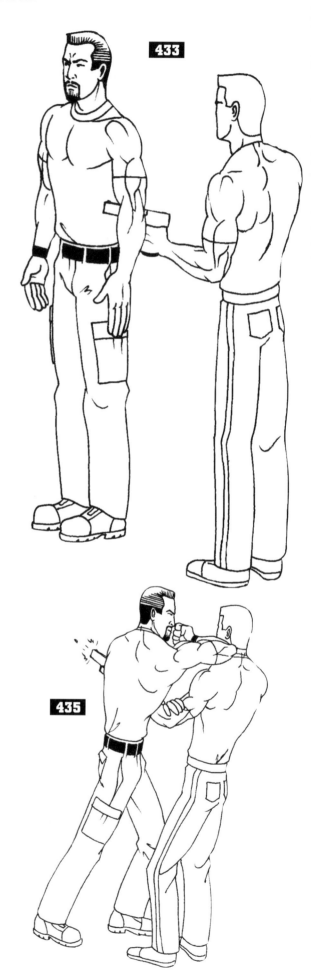

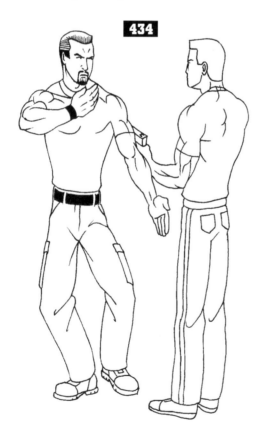

4. When you touch the gun, he will likely involuntarily shoot (discharge) it. Don't worry; you are out of the line of fire. Loud bang. Ears ringing. He is surprised because you caused the discharge and he didn't expect it. The sound will hurt. Your adrenaline will help you.

Gun Threat Side - Low - Side of Body - In Front Of The Arm

The gun is now **probably not jammed** because your hands did not necessarily touch the slide (or cylinder, if a revolver) and interfere with its operation. He may keep discharging the gun. Keep working.

5. As you step in and trap his arm (from #3 above) hit him with your free arm elbow as shown in **Picture 435**.

6. With your rear leg, knee him and step forcefully through him to disrupt his balance as shown in **Picture 436**. Do not pull your leg back upon striking with the knee, simply step forward pushing him back. Keep a strong grip with your trapping arm. Do not let the gun arm get loose.

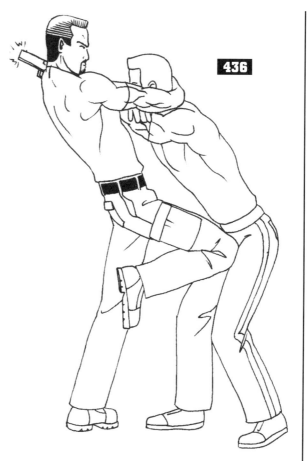

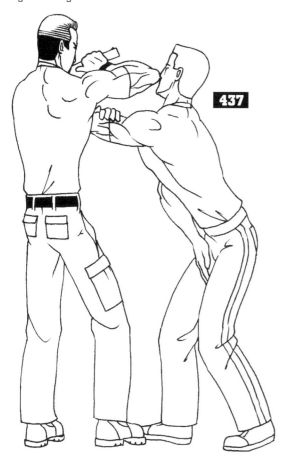

7. Reach over the gun with your free hand and grab the slide as shown in **Picture 437 and Picture 438**. Note the turned position of your hand with the thumb on the outside side of the gun. This position will give you the leverage necessary to break the gun free.

8. Twist your hand sharply 90 degrees and 'punch out' straight with the gun to take it away as shown in **Picture 438, 439 and 440**. Depending upon which hand he is using you may break his finger and rip off the skin.

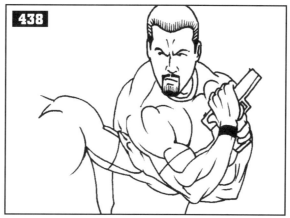

Gun Threat Side - Low - Side of Body - Behind The Arm

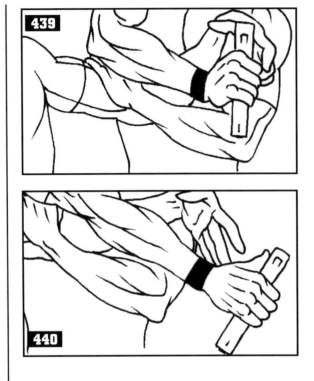

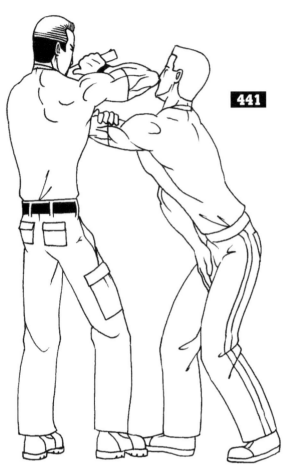

9. Deliver an elbow to the face as shown in **Picture 81**.

10. Take three steps back, rack the slide to clear the jam, and as shown in **Picture 442**, point the gun at him and tell him to get on the floor. It would be a good idea to glance at the gun and be sure the safety (if any) is off.

11. If he resumes his attack and you are in fear for your life (and a reasonable person would see the situation as you do), in most jurisdictions you are justified to shoot. Otherwise while he remains on the floor call the police or have someone else do so. When they arrive and likely draw their guns- do exactly as they say. They don't know who the bad guy really is. Do not under any circumstances point the gun in the direction of the police.

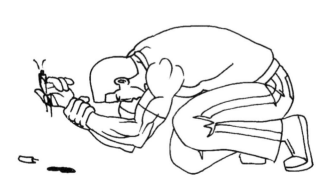

GUN THREAT- REAR – TOUCHING BODY OR HEAD

Primary Danger- Line of Fire (get out of it)

1. The attacker is standing behind you holding a gun pointed at your upper back, neck or head similar to **Picture 443 or 444**.

2. Comply. Begin your statement and raise your hands but keep them below the level of the gun, if you know it, otherwise not more than chest high as shown in **Picture 443**.

3. At about the middle of your compliance statement (after or as you say 'want'), rapidly turn toward the attacker and step in with your same side leg (passing the gun) and trap his gun arm by wrapping your arm under it as shown in **Picture 444 and 445**. You are out of the line of fire as soon as you have turned your body.

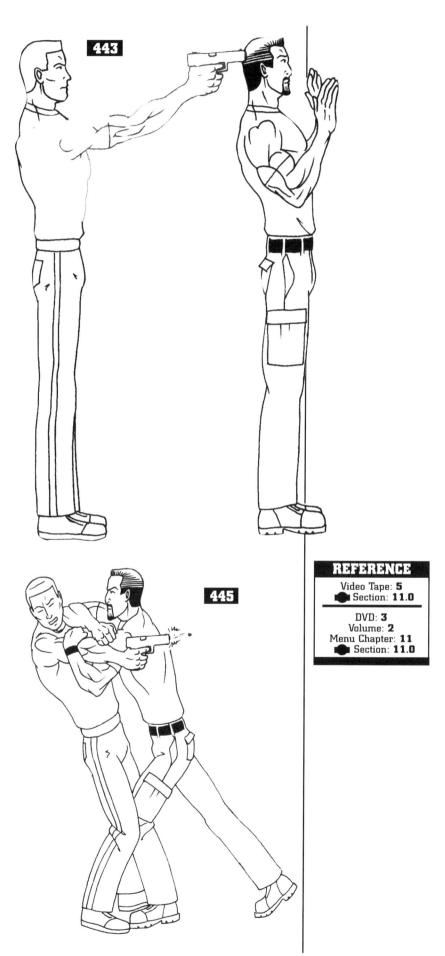

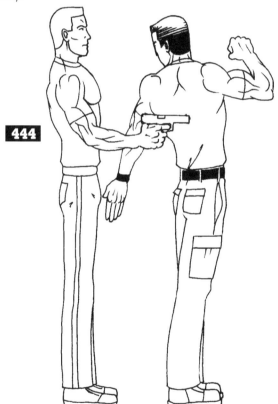

REFERENCE
Video Tape: **5**
Section: **11.0**

DVD: **3**
Volume: **2**
Menu Chapter: **11**
Section: **11.0**

4. When you touch the gun, he will likely involuntarily shoot (discharge) it. Don't worry; you are out of the line of fire. Loud bang. Ears ringing. But, he is surprised. You caused the discharge, he didn't expect it, and you did. The sound will hurt. Your adrenaline will help you. The gun is now probably not jammed because your hands didn't necessarily touch the slide (or cylinder if a revolver) and interfere with its operation. He may keep discharging the gun. Keep working.

Gun Threat Rear - High - Touching Body Or Head

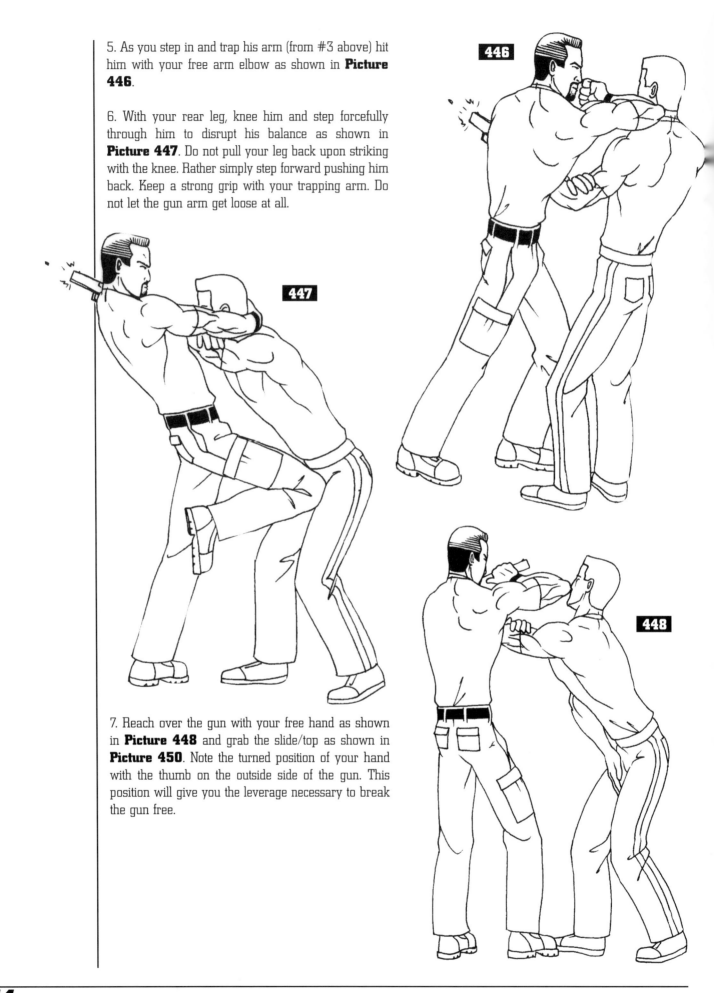

5. As you step in and trap his arm (from #3 above) hit him with your free arm elbow as shown in **Picture 446**.

6. With your rear leg, knee him and step forcefully through him to disrupt his balance as shown in **Picture 447**. Do not pull your leg back upon striking with the knee. Rather simply step forward pushing him back. Keep a strong grip with your trapping arm. Do not let the gun arm get loose at all.

446

447

7. Reach over the gun with your free hand as shown in **Picture 448** and grab the slide/top as shown in **Picture 450**. Note the turned position of your hand with the thumb on the outside side of the gun. This position will give you the leverage necessary to break the gun free.

448

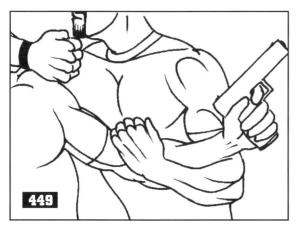

8. Twist your hand sharply 90 degrees and 'punch out' straight with the gun to take it away as shown in **Picture 451 and 452**. Depending upon which hand he is using you may break his finger and/or rip off the skin.

9. Deliver an elbow to the face.

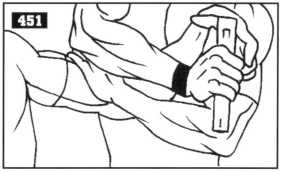

10. Take three steps back, rack the slide to clear the jam, and as shown in **Picture 453**, point the gun at him and tell him to get on the floor. It would be a good idea to glance at the gun and be sure the safety (if any) is off.

11. If he resumes his attack and you are in fear for your life (and a reasonable person would see the situation as you do), in most jurisdictions you are justified

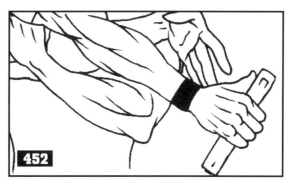

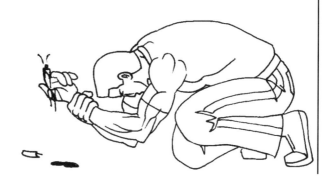

to shoot. Otherwise while he remains on the floor call the police or have someone do so. When they arrive and likely draw their guns- do exactly as they say. They don't know who the bad guy really is. Do not under any circumstances point the gun in the direction of the police.

Gun Threat - Rear - High - Hostage Style

REFERENCE
Video Tape: **5**
◼ Section: **12.0**

DVD: **3**
Volume: **2**
Menu Chapter: **12**
◼ Section: **12.0**

GUN THREAT – REAR –HOSTAGE STYLE

Primary Danger – Line of Fire

1. The attacker is standing behind you pointing the gun at the side of your head (or even a bit higher). He might put his other arm around your neck and/or grab your shirt with the other hand as shown in **Picture 454**. This is usually done when he is taking you hostage and intends to negotiate with someone else using you for leverage. The trick here is that you will not be able to get out of the line of fire by moving your head, because the gun will follow. Therefore, you must move the gun.

2. Comply. Begin your statement and raise your hands to just above shoulder height (ideally the center of your hand is at the same height as the barrel of the gun and your hands are about even with your face) as shown in **Picture 454**. Make sure your thumb and side of hand form a 90 degree angle (an 'L').

3. At about the middle of your compliance statement (after or as you say 'want'), rapidly turn your palm in the direction of your head. Your objective is to catch the gun under the trigger guard, close your hand and immediately turn it (and the gun) back around so that the gun is pointing forward as shown in **Picture 455 and 456**. For added protection, you can simultaneously turn your head away from the gun as you are turning it out. You are out of the line of fire as soon as the gun is half way to pointing forward.

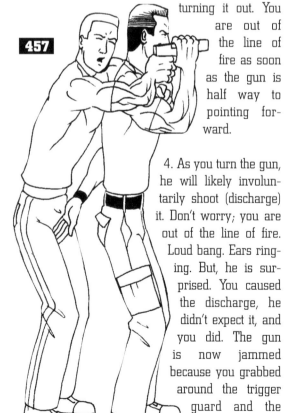

457

4. As you turn the gun, he will likely involuntarily shoot (discharge) it. Don't worry; you are out of the line of fire. Loud bang. Ears ringing. But, he is surprised. You caused the discharge, he didn't expect it, and you did. The gun is now jammed because you grabbed around the trigger guard and the

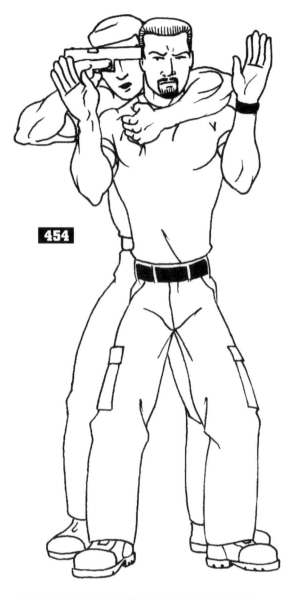

454

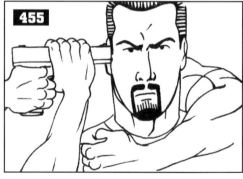

455

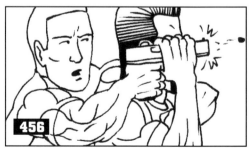

456

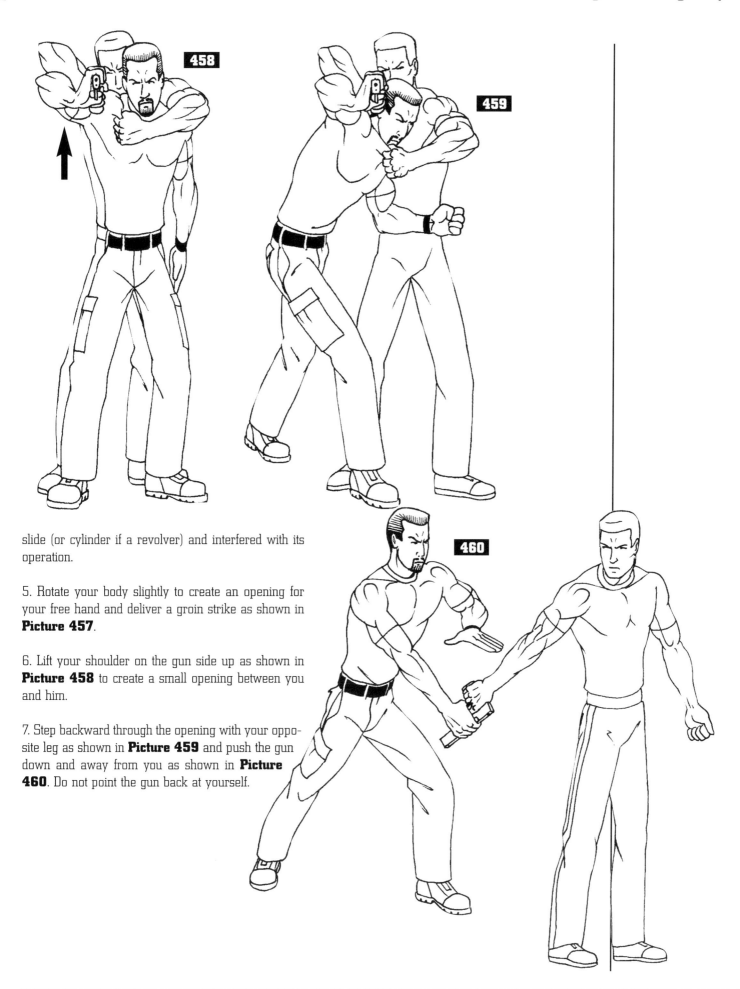

slide (or cylinder if a revolver) and interfered with its operation.

5. Rotate your body slightly to create an opening for your free hand and deliver a groin strike as shown in **Picture 457**.

6. Lift your shoulder on the gun side up as shown in **Picture 458** to create a small opening between you and him.

7. Step backward through the opening with your opposite leg as shown in **Picture 459** and push the gun down and away from you as shown in **Picture 460**. Do not point the gun back at yourself.

8. Form a 'V' with the thumb and side of your free hand as shown in **Picture 461** and turn it upside down and smash the attackers gun hand wrist while stepping back with your other leg. Hit as close to the wrist as possible or it may be difficult to remove the gun. The step backwards and downward pull on the gun will add leverage to the strike and will help free the gun.

9. Take three steps back, rack the slide to clear the jam, and as shown in **Picture 462**, point the gun at him and tell him to get on the floor. It would be a good idea to glance at the gun and be sure the safety (if any) is off.

10. If he resumes his attack and you are in fear for your life (and a reasonable person would see the situation as you do), in most jurisdictions you are justified to shoot. Otherwise while he remains on the floor call the police or have someone do so. When they arrive and likely draw their guns- do exactly as they say. They don't know who the bad guy really is. Do not under any circumstances point the gun in the direction of the police.

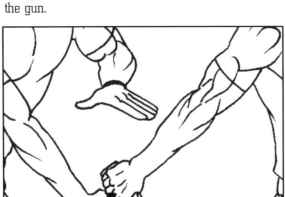

461

462

Index

Notes